A DANCE WITH LIFE

For Kate,

My sincere wishes.

John Gilpin

A Dance with Life

by

JOHN GILPIN

Foreword by
Sir Anton Dolin

WILLIAM KIMBER · LONDON

First published in 1982 by
WILLIAM KIMBER AND CO. LIMITED
Godolphin House, 22a Queen Anne's Gate,
London, SW1H 9AE

ISBN 0-7183-0408-X

Photoset by Robcroft Ltd, London WC1
and printed and bound in Great Britain by
The Garden City Press Limited,
Letchworth, Hertfordshire SG6 1JS

For my daughter Tracy, and
for Kay with gratitude.

I wish to acknowledge the tireless and indispensable help given to me by Kay Hunter in writing this book.

J.G.

Contents

List of Illustrations

Foreword
By Sir Anton Dolin

There are few – if any – more able to write a preface to this brave, fascinating book of John Gilpin's than I. I certainly have not known him as long as his wonderful mother, his twin brother Tony, or indeed the indestructible great lady of ballet, Dame Marie Rambert. I can claim more than thirty years of a remarkable friendship and artistic association, through many triumphs and a great many tribulations, all of which, to a great extent, I was a part of.

From the beginning of London's Festival Ballet John was its great shining star. Our first meeting was in Paris, at the Salle Pleyel. He was at that time a member of Le Grand Ballet de Marquis de Cuevas. The meeting was not exactly a congenial one, as he tells in his autobiography, though I do not remember kissing him on the lips as asked to by Marie Rambert – but what does it matter? I thought him, quite wrongly as it turned out, conceited, and in no way did I wish to be involved. Yet Fate and Ana Ricarda decided otherwise. For it was on her recommendation that I agreed, with Julian Braunsweg, to accept him as the leading dancer of the company I was forming at the end of 1949. It was a decision I have never regretted, and one I have very reason to be grateful for, artistically and personally in every way.

I have been his friend and he has been mine for over thirty years. It has been, especially over the last ten of those turbulent years, a period of wonderful mutual help, not always easy to give or accept, on his side in particular. For astrologically I am a Leo, in strong opposition to his Aquarius, and our stars crossed in no uncertain terms.

I have been with John on so many occasions, witnessed his wonderful bravery and his six ghastly operations on those dancing legs. Now he has written his book, bared himself almost naked to the world, and told the truth of his life with honesty and sincerity. I can say truthfully that John Gilpin is one of England's great dancers – but much more, he is a great human being, a man who has lived and survived a multitude of great adversities and conquered them all with strength and humility.

God gave him the gift of Dance, and the ability to achieve what he set out to do in life – give a dedicated service to the world of ballet, and find faith in himself.

ANTON DOLIN

Prologue

Nothing can change my destiny. It was, and is, already written. We never know what is around the next corner, and that is what is so exciting about life, yet my instincts seem to grow sharper as I grow older.

The last two weeks have been a revelation to me. Being alone in the quiet solitude and beauty of this place has made me look into myself and try to re-assess my life – where I am going and what I am about. Although I seem to be very happy at the moment, being here and alone, I keep going through periods of doubt and insecurity. Am I good enough for what lies ahead? Gone are the days of just getting up and doing things without thought for the consequences. As we grow older we know all the pitfalls from past experience. Sometimes I wish I had known earlier what I know now, but that is not how it was meant to be. All has to be learned from our triumphs and downfalls – if we ever learn.

Deep in my core I have always longed for freedom, vast space, endless horizons. Looking back, I see how much I did wrong, how much valuable time I wasted, purely from self-indulgence and selfishness. There is so much to learn and so little time. I must try to stop putting up barriers within myself, but due to my life I think that was a protection against being hurt and vulnerable.

Perhaps I am really running away from myself, yet we can only find freedom – whatever that is – within ourselves. We create all the obstacles that beset our paths, put up the barriers and excuses to attempt to smooth the way, but we fail.

I have such great hopes and expectations, yet I let unimportant things distract me from the main issue. Perhaps I am fundamentally lazy, although I am not aware of it. I have never seemed to be able to plan ahead like other people, but have just gone through life hoping there was always something good around the corner.

The only time I ever felt free was when I was on the stage, dancing. Now I no longer have that outlet. The end had to come, but it all happened so suddenly I did not know how to cope with it. I was shattered, hence my fall. There must have been a seed of self-destruction, but the will to survive pulled me through. I now know that whatever happens to me I will fight body and soul to keep alive. It is a 'plus' that I am still alive and have my legs. Also that I can still work.

I wonder what is the real motivation which leads me on to do the things I am doing. Is it just the desire to perform, and therefore selfish and egotistical? Or is it the love of it? I loved to dance – and still would – although I know that is impossible. But it will always be there, though time has passed. Yet time is a man-made thing. It does not exist in this great Universe. It goes on beyond eternity.

I believe whatever power created mankind, there is one great force on this planet. Whatever comes, our lives are nothing in the great pattern. Through my own very personal and awe-inspiring spiritual experiences I know there is something far beyond the comprehension of man. We are like infants, blind to the knowledge of what the human brain is capable. Perhaps by the end of my life I will understand just a little more.

I wake each morning with a feeling of expectation, wondering what might happen this day. I begin to dream again. In the quiet and tranquillity of this place, at this very moment the music of the Fauré Requiem is pouring forth. How beautiful and peaceful it is. Music to me is one of the God given gifts to man. I would have loved to be a great musician and singer, but I was made to interpret music through my mind and body. That is enough to ask.

But how and where did it all begin, this destiny of mine? As I sit here alone I find myself going back to childhood, thinking about my beautiful Devonshire . . .

J.G.
Newfoundland, 1981

Chapter One

I could see myself from top to toe in that magic mirror in my grandmother's bedroom.

When I danced and posed in front of it, the small boy on the other side looked back at me and did exactly as I did. He was me, but it was like looking at somebody else. My twin brother perhaps? No, my twin brother did not look like a reflection of me. We were not identical, and he knew nothing about the magic mirror. Nobody knew. When I was alone I would rush upstairs and dance for the boy on the other side of the mirror – and for myself because I had to. Narcissus-like, I loved to watch the reflection, fascinated by my own movements and the things I could do with my feet and arms.

I was three years old at the time.

So often I have been asked who, or what made me want to dance, and it is impossible to give a conclusive answer. It is like asking a man why he had to climb a mountain and being told, 'Because it was there.' For me, dancing was always 'there' as far back as I can remember. How it came to be there I cannot say. My mother always loved ballroom dancing and was very good at it, so I may have been endowed with a pre-natal gift for music and movement which was to remain with me for ever. Unlike The Sleeping Beauty, who was to play a part in my later life, I had no good fairies at my christening likely to have granted me a gift from Terpischore, nor was I inspired by seeing a famous dancer. Indeed, the first ballet I ever saw was when I was eight, when Sadlers-Wells came to Exeter. By that time I was already studying dancing.

The principal male dancer at that performance was Robert Helpmann, and the very first ballet I ever saw was *Les Sylphides*.

My mother was with me, and I think my dancing teacher, and I recall being taken backstage after the performance. One of the impressive things about Robert Helpmann was his stage make-up, which was always immaculate, but by today's standards very heavy. On this occasion he was wearing a wig, his black-lined eyes were enormous, and a carmine mouth appeared to go on for ever.

'Good Heavens, John,' said my mother afterwards. 'If you become a dancer I hope you won't go around like that!'

My love of dance was fundamental, and even as a toddler I had only to hear music and I would hop, skip and jump around, unable to stop myself. 'John never walked,' my mother has told people on many occasions. So I danced my way through childhood, which was very happy, despite the fact it was rather unsettled and the early years littered with numerous changes of residence. We moved, seemingly relentlessly, from one south coast naval town to another, according to the dictates of the Royal Navy as we followed in the wake of my father. He was William John Gilpin, a sailor before and during the last war. A Londoner by birth, from Walthamstow, his original roots were in the far north, stretching back into Cumbria and Northumbria, the earliest records being in the Lake District. He joined the Royal Navy in 1928, and from then on family life became nomadic.

My mother, Lilian May Lendon, came from quite the opposite end of England. Her family were all from the south-west, and she was born in Newton Abbot, Devonshire. Mother was the eldest of six children, and at the age of fourteen had to go out into service to help support the rest of the family. Although I may have been born with dancing shoes on my feet, there is no question of having been born with a silver spoon in my mouth.

My twin brother Tony and I were born in Southsea, Hampshire, on 10th February 1930, and nature dictated that my mother remained in one place long enough to play her part in that major event. I was born first, and was the smaller, weaker twin. It was thought shortly after my birth that I might not survive, and the doctor dispensed encouragement to my mother by saying, 'Never mind – you still have another one.' But it seemed I had a great grip on life even at that early age, and I came through the first of my many survival tests, determined to hang on at all costs.

It was not long before the now enlarged family was on the move again. Over the next few years we found ourselves deposited in such maritime centres as Devonport, Chatham, Plymouth, and wherever

(*Left*) My mother. A photograph taken in 1935. (*Right*) My father in Royal Navy uniform, 1932

My parents' wedding day, 1928, with (left to right) my father's and mother's parents.

With mother and Tony, Sidmouth, 1934

Tony and me with our father on the beach at Dawlish, 1932

(*Above*) In our own transport at home at Dawlish, 1933.

(*Left*) With Tony on our uncle's motor bike and sidecar, 1933.

my father happened to be stationed while he was serving on cruisers. Our mother claims to have lost count of the number of times her furniture was put into store as a result of our unsettled existence. Because her family was all in the west country it was to Devonshire that we gravitated during our father's often long absences at sea, and Dawlish became our home town. Sometimes months went by with no communication from Father, and we would discover later that he had been on the Russian or Atlantic convoys. Most of the time we never knew where he was, and he was an elusive figure during our childhood, only seen when he came on leave.

Both parents were strict but loving, and although there was not a lot of money we were brought up very well. My early dancing lessons with good teachers meant a big sacrifice for my parents, for which I am eternally grateful. They never stood in my way, but even if there had been opposition I know I would have done it all myself later. As it was, everything fell into place, like a giant jig-saw puzzle where everything fits exactly.

It was later to be my father's lot to sail under the sea rather than on it when he became a submarine commander. On one occasion during the war his ship was reported missing, and for six months we heard nothing. There was great anguish in the family until we learned that his vessel had been torpedoed and he was transferred to another ship. As a result of an injury to his spine when he was in Malta he was eventually invalided out of the navy. He was never one to talk about his wartime experiences or regale one with anecdotes, so it is with sadness and a certain surprise that I now realise how little I knew of him in those days. Throughout our early childhood the circumstances made it impossible for him to spend much time with my brother and myself. To a great extent we grew up without him, and now from my own age of maturity I sense that perhaps he resented the fact that he missed out so much on our early upbringing. It was marvellous when he was at home, but then he would disappear again for months on end, and during his absence the various stages of family life went on, with their minor day-to-day happenings and major crises, all of which he was not there to witness or be part of. It was a situation which must have been repeated in thousands of homes during the war, responsible for so many break-ups and partings.

Our first move as a family was from Southsea to Plymouth, and all my earliest memories are of life in the west country, in the company of my mother's family. Because of that, reminiscences of that side of the family are more valid than those of my father's family. One of my clearest recollections is that of my maternal grandmother, the one who owned the mirror. A fragile-looking, beautiful woman, she was notably graceful, and I always used to think of her as The Grey Lady because of the grey, misty chiffon colours she used to wear. I needed no encouragement to dance, but I suppose she played at least some part in the development of my natural talent.

It was an uncalculated encouragement, and certainly not with any idea of promoting a theatrical career. I was far too young, and anyway such a contingency had never been contemplated. There was no history of professional theatre in the family, and at that time there was no reason to suppose that I would be the first member to take to the boards. Both our parents were musical. Apart from my mother's expertise at ballroom dancing, my father could play the violin quite well, but there had never been any aspirations towards professionalism. Somehow that was going to be left to me. It was as though my future had already been written; nothing really occurred by chance, if indeed it ever does.

When I went to visit my grandmother she would put on gramophone records so that I could dance for her, both of us delighting in what were then no more than untrained infant caperings. My grandfather was a kind, gentle man who worked on the Great Western Railway, and although I can recall him during those early years, it was my grandmother who has left the most vivid impression.

Apart from our frequent moves we had a fairly normal, closely knit family background. Because we always lived on the coast we spent a lot of time on the beaches in summer. We also had family outings, often to Dartmoor or other beauty spots, and I developed a deep love for Devonshire. How lucky I was to have been brought up amid such beautiful surroundings, with the coast and moorlands – to the south cosy and picturesque, to the north wild and free. I often imagined myself living right in the heart of the moors, quite wild and savage, with nothing to bother about but simply existing. That was one of my dream worlds which I inhabited. I had several. Whenever we were taken to Dartmoor I would wander off to some secluded ravine or gully, with the fast moving water of the moorland streams, and instantly I summoned up my make-believe world.

I was an adventurer or explorer, treading undiscovered land. I always felt very close to nature and loved the wildness of it all. I would drop into pools and let the water pour over me – icy but exciting, at the same time being intensely aware of what might suddenly appear out of the trees in that imaginary, but very real tropical bush or jungle . . . I am not sure what I was waiting for, but it had to be something or somebody magic. So I guess my fantasies began very early. At times when I look into myself it seems that all my life I have either been seeking freedom or running away from something.

Travel was like a drug, and is still, to this day. I must be on the move, and yet I could never be totally without roots. I must always have a base, both to return to and escape from. When I was still quite young in Devonshire I acquired an additional means of travel outside the family picnic perimeter. A friend of my mother's family, whose daughter was at Infant School and dancing class with me, ran a tourist bus during the summer months. Whenever I could do so I would ride with him, sitting beside him when he made trips to such places as Clovelly and Haytor. This mode of transport enabled me to see much of the whole lovely county, almost from end to end.

Although I was a seasoned traveller in my own country from an early age, there came an unexpected bonus in 1935 in the form of a visit to Malta. My father had been stationed there with the Mediterranean fleet, and we were to follow. On the way to Plymouth to board the ship my brother and I were in a state of high excitement, a feeling unshared by our long-suffering mother. Not only was she having to move again, and get herself and two small sons across the ocean, but she was a notoriously bad sea traveller and viewed the whole venture with trepidation, with the result that she was almost sea-sick before she was up the gangway of the P & O liner which was to take us! Certainly from the time she set foot on deck she was stricken hopelessly by the miserable *mal de mer*, a condition which remained with her for the rest of the voyage, rendering her unfit to leave the ship's sick bay for the entire trip.

As if one patient in the family was not enough, my brother saw fit to add to the Gilpin casualty list by shutting his thumb in a cabin door. He too was removed to sick bay, leaving me as the sole survivor. Just to prove that things don't always happen in threes, I remained unscathed, and thoroughly enjoyed the attention which came my way from sympathetic fellow travellers. Cosseted, amused and entertained by the staff on board, I was beautifully looked after and had a marvellous time all by myself. Perhaps I was the only member of the family who was sorry to come to the end of the voyage!

The boat docked in the Grand Harbour at Valetta, and I remember my first sight of the women in their black dresses, with veils over their heads. Our new, albeit temporary home was in Sliema, just outside Valetta, where my father had taken a house. Yet another waterfront, but this time in warmer climes than the English naval bases, and the house had a magnificent view over the Grand Harbour. We were in Malta at the time of the Silver Jubilee of King George V and Queen Mary in 1935, and as part of the celebrations the whole fleet in the Grand Harbour was lit up, the outlines of the ships picked out with thousands of light bulbs. It was the most wonderful fairylike sight.

Up to the time of going to Malta Tony and I had not attended school because we were not old enough. I have some hazy recollections of going to the Royal Navy children's school in Malta, obviously not sufficiently impressive to have left its mark. But I do recall being a guest at some wonderful Royal Navy children's parties while we were on the island.

Some memories remain of the eight months we spent there, one not unnaturally connected with dancing, and an impromptu performance I gave to a captive audience seeking nothing more than a peaceful Sunday afternoon, uninterrupted by a precocious display by a pocket Nijinsky.

The Royal Naval Band played on a Sunday afternoon on the large park-like area overlooking the Grand Harbour. We were often taken for walks there, and the music floated across among the tables and chairs set out on the grass. One particular Sunday there was the usual gathering around the bandstand, including my parents, Tony and myself. I have no recollection of the piece of music which prompted my performance, and indeed only vaguely remember the whole incident, but my mother recalls it vividly. As always, it was impossible for me to keep my feet still under the influence of music, and I was suddenly impressed to dance, right there among all those people, unselfconsciously weaving my way around the tables, interpreting the music as I saw fit. There was no stopping me until the piece of music ended, by which time all heads had turned towards me. After a split second's silence I received an indulgent burst of applause, much to my father's embarrassment.

What I remember of Malta are the hot Mediterranean days and warm blissful nights. Rocks and sand and an azure sea, with every day like a holiday. Even at that early age I remember being aware of the amazing number of churches on the island, and that they were all Roman Catholic. It was in Malta that Tony and I learned to swim, in the hospitable Mediterranean. We both loved the water, and our father took us to the sea when he was off duty. There was no beach, only rocks leading to quite deep water of a very blue sea. Father would tie rubber rings around us and simply throw us in, whereupon we would flap and paddle around like ducks, bobbing up to the surface.

One day he threw us in without the rubber rings and somehow we just swam. I suppose many children would have been terrified and subject to panic, but for some reason we weren't. I have loved swimming ever since, and of course it is one of the few exercises which does no harm to a dancer. The sea has always played a part in my life, and I am never so happy as when I am near it or in it. If ever I buy another house of my own I would want it to be near the water. I revel in storms and tempests at sea, but to me all nature is beautiful in every season. I am equally moved by hot deserts and cool valleys, mountains and forests, and was very fortunate in later life that my profession enabled me to experience all climates, all geographical wonders throughout the world.

Malta was my initiation to foreign travel, and we lived there in a row of houses built on the side of a hill. The houses had flat roofs and steps up the outside, leading to the roofs. In front was a kind of scrubland where goats grazed, and an area of enormous stinging nettles five or six feet high. Tony, wearing only a pair of shorts, once had the misfortune to fall into the bed of mammoth nettles and was literally covered with stings from head to foot, which must have been agonising.

Like Shakespeare's magic island in *The Tempest*, Malta was 'full of noises', and there was an occasion when Tony and I made our own contribution to the local activities. Our parents had gone out, but my mother, being reminded of the occasion, assures me they had only gone out to buy ice cream, and certainly we were never left alone for any length of time. There was always somebody with us, but on that occasion the isolation felt as though it was going on for hours.

I have no idea what woke us up, but wake we did, somehow realising that the house was silent, and that it must be very late, even though it probably was not. We went downstairs only to discover there was nobody at home. A sense of isolation gripped us, and in sheer panic we went on to the doorstep and starting crying and screaming our heads off. All the Maltese neighbours materialised as if from nowhere, and there a great to-do because we seemed to have succeeded in rousing the whole street. The family-conscious Maltese were highly indignant that we had been left alone, and we were taken into the next door house to calm us down. When our parents returned home they were frantic to discover we were not in our beds and missing from the house. When we were eventually located there were explanations made all round, and I don't think we were at all popular for having caused such a commotion and embarrassment.

I went to Malta in 1973 for a holiday, and tried to find the places I had known as a child, but it had changed greatly and was rather sad. It is always at great peril to our memories that we return to scenes of childhood. Nothing remains the same; houses which seemed huge when we were children have suddenly shrunk, housing estates stand on our wild playgrounds, and the entire backdrop has changed, as though we had walked on to the set of an unfamiliar play. In Malta I found the great dockyards run down, and I had a feeling of claustrophobia, although it is still a lovely island with many untouched magnificent churches of all sizes.

We left Malta at the time of the outbreak of the Abyssinian war, and my father was moved to another part of the world. The move coincided with the point when our formal education had to be considered, and when we returned to Devonshire Tony and I started school at the Infant School in Dawlish.

I think I quite enjoyed it, what little I can remember of it, but I was never a good academic pupil even in my later schooldays. Lessons had to mean something. I was always interested in history and geography, and subjects which somehow came alive, but such things as mathematics left me cold. Tony had a grasp of formal lessons which exceeded mine, and he was always slightly ahead of me. He and I are different in many ways. Physically we are not by any means identical twins, but emotionally and artistically we are very much alike. We grew apart quickly and at an early age simply because circumstances forced us into different directions. We were only at school together until the age of nine, when I went to the Arts Educational School. Tony never had any desire to dance. He was a good footballer, playing for Chelsea youth team before he went into the RAF as a radar operator. His artistic leanings emerged into music, and he became an excellent musician.

Our early schooldays were exactly like those of other children, and at that stage we had no idea our paths would divide before we were very much older. I was not a particularly strong child, and my mother was advised to allow me to take up some form of athletic activity with the hope of building up my stamina. In view of my apparent interest in music and dancing, the obvious answer appeared to be for me to attend dancing lessons, so Mother arranged this against considerable opposition from my father's side of the family. Because Father was away from home, any decisions had to be made by our mother, and they became her responsibility. At that time it was very rare for a boy to indulge in such pursuits as dancing classes, which were thought of as purely feminine preserves. Little girls went to dancing classes, but little boys did not; they played football and cricket, fought in the playground, played soldiers, and wanted to be engine drivers. It seemed to the conventional members of my father's family that sending me to dancing classes was tantamount to putting me into skirts. What on earth could my mother be thinking about, they wondered, to allow me to be emasculated in that way? In their own peculiar way I think they felt almost sorry for me that I was being guided on the wrong lines in my father's absence. It was all part of the age-old prejudice against any alteration to the fixed roles of male and female, and the mistaken theory that all male dancers are effeminate. Little heed is paid to the fact that dancing is physically one of the toughest professions, just as demanding as the life of a footballer or athlete. My mother was convinced she was right in allowing me to take up dancing lessons, and time proved that her very difficult decision was totally justified. Even at the time of my first lessons there was still no driving theatrical ambition on my mother's part to push me on to the stage. That was something which came to me naturally as I progressed.

We were living in Gosport at the time, another naval move having taken place, and Mother made enquiries as to the whereabouts of a good dancing teacher. Her quest led her to Tina Pearce of Southsea, who became my first teacher. Her classes were to be taken seriously and were conducted in a strictly professional style. Even at my young age I was aware of her quality, and of the fact that this was something rather special and not just a run of the mill childish dancing class. Tina Pearce had a classical head and long neck, and I'm sure she could have become a great dancer. What beautiful line and style she had, and how patient she was with one so young.

From the moment I began to learn to dance properly I knew that this was the only thing I had ever wanted to do. Those beginnings were so valuable, as indeed are any child's first dancing lessons. For me, they put me on the right road, with high ideals of what dance was, and was to become in my life. It is about tremendous endurance and great joy. It is also about hard work, which is the trite warning issued to every youngster who wants to go on the stage, but the physical demands of the ballet world are extremely tough. When I look back I realise that although I was only seven years old, there were considerable efforts to be made and difficulties to overcome in even getting to my dancing class, let alone the energy I expended when I arrived there. Twice a week I had to make a grand safari, taking the ferry from Gosport to Portsmouth, then a bus to Southsea, where I had a ballet lesson from Tina Pearce and a tap lesson from a Mrs Walker, and then I would make the return trip.

When my father was at home he used to meet me at the bus stop on my return journey. He had a saddle on the crossbar of his bicycle, and I would climb up on to it and ride home with him. I suppose I must have been quite tired, but I never noticed because I loved going to dancing classes, which were the highlight of the week, and would have cheerfully undertaken a journey twice as long in order to get there.

In 1937 my father went to Chatham for posting, which meant another move for us. Off went the entire family to Chatham, and after my father left, my mother, Tony and I returned to Devonshire, where I came under the wing of my second teacher, Barbara Spencer-Edwards, who ran a dancing school in Teignmouth.

Fortunately she too was an excellent mentor, and I started to work in earnest for the British Ballet Organisation Grades, taking Number 1 and skipping to Elementary. In addition to ballet I was doing tap, musical comedy and acrobatic dancing, not realising then that acrobatics were not particularly good for ballet. As soon as it was pronounced unsuitable, I gave it up and concentrated on the other aspects. Both teachers gave me a good first grounding which is so important to the beginner, because many potentially good dancers have been ruined by bad training in the early years.

The dancing school used to give the usual concerts and annual displays, and there were three small girls I always partnered at that time, but the one I danced with most was a girl called Anne Baulkwell, whose father had a farm at Holcombe. I was very small for my age, and often had cause to be grateful to my protective twin brother, who rescued me from several scraps. Naturally, I had to put up with the general reaction to a boy who attended dancing classes.

'Your brother's a silly sissy!' was a typical ribald jibe often directed at Tony, who would promptly launch into an affray in my defence, although I think much of the teasing went over my head.

A glance at the family album shows me in various guises at performances given by the dancing school. I faced the audiences as a Quaker boy, together with Anne Baulkwell as a Quaker girl. There is another snapshot of me, gracefully posed in the company of my ringleted partner, complete with her hair ribbons and Shirley Temple style dress, and it seems I even 'blacked up' on one occasion. We often performed in local talent displays at Dawlish, in a marquee graced by the usual seaside Follies.

The seaside played a large part in our lives. Summers seemed long, if not endless when one was young, and with the beach almost on our doorstep, hot days and blue skies were infinite. Statistics on the weather never seem to bear out what one remembers. Surely our summer holidays were never ruined by rain? Every day appeared to dawn sunny and hot – one could plan a picnic a week in advance and know that because it was August it would surely be fine. We had a beach hut, and spent the whole of the summers amid sea and sand,

and a background of the Dawlish gardens climbing upwards into the town. Tony and I were 'water babies', always in the sea, once being rescued from a watery grave when we were jumping into the sea from a breakwater. After leaping into a rapidly advancing tide, we were scooped up by a man who fortunately saw the danger. He grabbed us, one under each arm, and carried us to safety, the whole exercise at considerable expense to our mother's nerves.

As my dancing progressed I developed a fear of anything happening to my legs, with the result that I dreaded football, and always got out of it if I could. The only leg damage I sustained in those early days was when Tony threw a penknife towards my feet. It bounced off the ground and caught my leg, making quite a deep cut. I decided not to tell my mother about it, and she only found out after the wound went septic through lack of attention.

Dancing lessons and appearances in local shows led to something on a larger scale, and I was entered in the Sunshine Music Festival at Portsmouth Guildhall. It was shortly before my father left for the Far East, and he attended the event. Perhaps any misgivings he may have had were dispelled that particular evening because having entered in all divisions – tap, musical comedy, acrobatic, song and dance, and operatic ballet, as it was then called, I won five gold medals! My mother's decision to have me taught dancing was already beginning to pay off.

Although she has always been proud of my subsequent achievements she has never been a typical 'Ballet Mother', a species to be found sitting around at dancing lessons and pushing offspring into the limelight. Ballet Mothers often had dancing aspirations themselves, and therefore wish to see their daughters achieve what they could not, so they become over-ambitious. Some very famous dancers have mothers who go on guiding and advising their children for the rest of their professional lives. Two Ballet Mothers were on tour with us with Festival Ballet – Tamara Toumanova's mother and Violette Verdy's mother. Both thought their respective daughters unsurpassable and therefore there was no love lost between them, with sometimes unexpected and often quite funny results.

My own mother was self-effacing, and kept herself apart from any potential she-dragons who crossed her path as a result of my dancing. She never interfered with my training in any way, and although she toured with me in my first play, and my first Rambert tour, it was simply because of my age, and not because she wished to keep an eye on my progress.

A milestone in my life came in 1938, when I was entered for the Plymouth Society of Music Competition Festival. One of the judges was Olive Ripman, and according to the local paper, she was not over-impressed with the standard, but apparently noticed me. The newspaper cutting, which I still have, states:

> Miss Olive Ripman criticised operatic dancing classes at the Plymouth Society of Music Competition Festival. She said the feet were generally quite good, then upwards it began to get worse. 'Style in ballet dancing is most important,' she said. 'That, I find is lacking in those two classes. I would say that generally speaking, the footwork is good and the general style is poor.'
>
> She praised the work of eight-year-old John Gilpin of Teignmouth, who won the Operatic Dance Class for the Under Tens. His work, she said, 'showed exceptional promise.' John Gilpin also won the Tap Dancing for the Under-Tens, in which there were forty-nine entries, and won the Character and National Classes. He came second in the Song and Dance Class.

Another newspaper photograph of the time shows me doing a tap number complete with top hat and tails, in an entertainment given by the Barbara Spencer-Edwards School of Dancing, and with the caption 'Teignmouth's Fred Astaire'.

At its worst, this sort of event is, I suppose, unashamed 'pot-hunting', but at its best is a measure of the inescapable competitive element which any dancer faces in a professional career. Discouragement at a young age can often taken on the guise of cruelty, but can also be the kindest thing in the long run. The percentage of young products of the average dancing school who actually 'make it' professionally is sadly small, but necessarily so.

I was very fortunate in catching the eye of Olive Ripman, who approached my mother with the offer of a scholarship for me to the Cone-Ripman School. Dear Olive – she took a great interest in my activities all my life and was a great friend until the time of her death on 29th April, 1981, at the great age of ninety-four. What an amazing woman she was – highly intelligent, with tremendous taste, and a great believer in the quality of line plus musicality in a dancer. From the moment she saw my potential as a dancer she had great faith in me. Her encouragement gave me the right path to follow and the right priorities. All through my career I have thought of her and thanked her from the bottom of my heart.

Looking back, I realise how much I owe to so many great teachers whose classes I have attended during my life as a dancer.

I was fortunate to have been a pupil of Vera Volkova during her short time in London. What more can be said which has not already been said of this superb teacher? Quiet, shy, with never a raised voice. Just a quiet correction in one's ear and everything came right. Vera Volkova was one of the great teachers of this century – a pupil of Vaganova, with all the great Russian Schools behind her, she was a joy to work with, and could ask a pupil to do anything, even the most impossible things – and it became possible. If only England had kept her longer our ballet would have been richer. Instead she went to Denmark, and their gain was our loss. She taught me simplicity and the true beauty of the dance, musicality and line, as well as the intellectual thought behind it. But above all she taught me humility. How much she gave to the dancers of the world who had the privilege to work with her. Alas, she is no longer with us, but her great contribution will be there for ever.

Of the other teachers, two have given me personally so much of themselves – Nora Kiss in Paris when I was with Roland Petit, and Eileen Ward later when I was with Festival Ballet. But I have had wonderful opportunities of working with many of the greats – Preobrajenska, Volinine, Lepeshinskaya, Dudinskaya, Tchernicheva. And in my formative years one of the finest English teachers, Marion Knight, who taught me more than almost any teacher I had.

It is through such people as these that the great tradition of the ballet is handed down, and my quest to be part of this tradition began with Olive Ripman, who singled me out for her school.

The Cone-Ripman School was then in London, and the scholarship offer posed my mother with yet another major decision at a time when my father was abroad. Having fought and survived the previous opposition from his family, she was faced with an even bigger dilemma. If the offer was accepted it meant I would be sent to

London, and there was a suspicion of my becoming a professional dancer, which was unheard of, and slightly outrageous. My father's side of the family did not really want to know about my dancing until I started to make a name for myself, when they became quite proud of me, but this is not unusual in families where there has never been any theatrical tradition. My mother was convinced it was right that I should take advantage of the scholarship, so I was allowed to go.

I went alone to London, stayed with my mother's sister in Balham, and went daily to the Ripman School in Baker Street. The Cone School was then over Lilley and Skinner's in Oxford Street. Shortly after the outbreak of war in 1939 the whole school was evacuated to a beautiful house called The Hallams in Shamley Green, near Guildford. My mother took a small flat in Guildford, bringing Tony with her, and I commuted each day from there. I found myself the only boy among 200 girls. Although there were boys at the London school, I was the only one at Guildford, but as far as I can recall it never bothered me nor caused me any embarrassment. I was far too interested in what I was doing. We did academic work in the mornings and dancing and theatrical work in the afternoons. The Cone sisters were pioneers of that type of schooling, and what marvellous women they were. Grace, Valerie and Lillie Cone had started a dancing school in Cricklewood, then Grace and Lillie gave classes in a church hall in Brighton, where Anton Dolin and Evelyn Laye were among their early pupils. In the thirties Olive Ripman, a great Cecchetti teacher, ballroom dancer and judge, joined them and together they formed the Cone-Ripman School, the first comprehensive performing arts school in the country.

Of the Cone sisters Grace was the driving force on the dancing side, and a very great teacher. Valerie, the eldest, who is now ninety-two, was the financial wizard, and then there was Lillie, who was also a fine teacher. One takes such people for granted when one is young, and it is not until later in life the realisation comes of the contribution they have made, both to the arts in general, and to so many careers.

The Hallams was a large Tudor house set in magnificent grounds, which lent themselves to the dancing displays we used to give at the end of term on the lawns. I recall doing a Greek dance, complete with reed pipes and dressed in a leopard skin. Parents often found it difficult to attend our displays because the blitzes had started and travelling was neither easy nor safe. Guildford was in direct line when the German bombers came over to attack London, and those who saw it will never forget the sight of the Hog's Back, completely ablaze with incendiary bombs. Air raid sirens whined day and night, and we began to take them for granted.

The house was set up very high near Shamley Green, amid a lot of pine woods. One day as I was walking along I kicked something metallic. Stooping to pick it up I realised it was a strange coin with the outline of a head on it. It was obviously extremely old, and I got quite excited about it, convinced I had made a great find. I took my discovery to the British Museum and was told, to my great delight, that the coin dated from the reign of Caesar Augustus, and that The Hallams was on the site of The Pilgrim's Way.

At the beginning of 1940 the whole school was going to be evacuated to America, the operation being sponsored by a group of theatre people in the States, some with associations with the Cone-Ripman School. Anton Dolin, a former Cone pupil, was one of them, and such famous personalities as Gertrude Lawrence, Noël Coward and Beatrice Lillie were also among those with a hand in proceedings. There was a great deal of anxiety at the time because we were even suffering from land mines coming down near the school, and sometimes we would see them descend on their parachutes, to explode as they hit the ground. It seemed that the sooner we all crossed the Atlantic the safer we would be. It was planned that Tony would come with me to the States, as Mother did not wish us to be parted, and we had even gone so far as to get our passports. Shortly before we were due to leave, news came through of the sinking of the SS *City of Benares*, the liner which was tragically torpedoed in the Atlantic while taking ninety British children to North America. Most of the passengers and crew died, and only thirteen of the child evacuees were saved, with the result that all overseas evacuation schemes were halted for a time, and I stayed on at The Hallams.

It was a temporary sojourn brought to an abrupt end when the army moved in and took over the house. I remember feeling a tremendous sense of shock as they drove through the beautiful old grounds with their lorries and tanks. Suddenly the war seemed to have come to our doorstep, and we were moved out. It was sad to leave that ancient house, with its hundreds of years of history, and an abiding childhood memory is that of seeing the old lawns ruthlessly ploughed into by heavy army vehicles. It seemed so callous and uncaring, but that was the nature of war, and compared with children in other European countries we were leading a charmed existence.

The army invasion added another excitement to our school life, and we were all bundled into buses and taken to our next stopping-off point, which was Loddington Hall in Rutland, right in the middle of England – isolated, and three miles from the nearest railway station of East Norton. Loddington Hall was another 'stately home', and again in lovely grounds. When we arrived most of the furniture had been moved out, and the rest was removed as the school took over. One can now perhaps imagine the owners' dismay at having to move the priceless family antiques and heirlooms as busloads of seemingly awful children took over the house.

Life at our new abode seemed too enjoyable to be 'school' and there was an air of being permanently on holiday, although in fact we worked very hard. Happily, there was no feeling of being under pressure. Life was geared towards the theatre and dancing, and although it was inevitable that many fell by the wayside, never to end up on the stage, there were others who went on to make a name for themselves. One of my contemporaries at Loddington Hall was Gillian Lynne, who became a highly successful dancer at the then Sadlers-Wells Ballet, and later she became a director and choreographer. I realise now what a privilege it was to have been allowed to specialise in a chosen subject the way we did. We all became like members of a large family, and the realities of war seemed far off as we worked and played in a lovely country atmosphere, almost unaware of what was going on in the troubled world outside. It is always so easy to look back and see the best in everything, and I am sure there must have been some bad times, but the memory retained is of happiness and satisfaction, and it is not everyone who can look back on schooldays with such affection.

At some stage during our stay there another boy arrived on the scene, and I quite welcomed his presence in the all-female community in which I found myself. The new arrival's name was Michael Absalom, and he too came from the south-west of England, from somewhere near Taunton in Somerset. There was a Polish matron at the school, Leah Kotashek, who had escaped from her own country when the Germans invaded. She mothered and spoiled Michael and me because we were in the minority, and because motherly women have a weakness for little boys far from home. Later two more boys arrived, and we were given a whole floor to ourselves in a side wing of the great house.

Michael, who was nine when he arrived, was a year younger than I was, so when it came to the time of going home for the holidays I was always deputed to look after him. Not only was I his senior by a year, but I also had the advantage of being an 'old resident' at Loddington Hall, which gave me the added status of being thought to be terribly responsible, and I think I probably was. Certainly I was never afraid of travelling alone, and did not give the matter a second thought. It was a tremendously long journey from Rutland to the south-west. We had to leave school at about six o'clock in the morning to get to the nearest station of East Norton. From there we went to Melton Mowbray for a train to St Pancras, and crossed London by tube to Paddington, from where we caught the train to Somerset and Devon. It was quite a daunting trip for a ten-year-old when I think about it now, but my early travels afforded good practice for the tours around the world which I was to make some years later. As I look back, it seems I have been travelling all my life in one way or another.

Michael and I must have presented a strange picture as we made our way home. I was small for my age, and I recall that he was even smaller. There was I with my suitcase, supervising this infant who not only carried his luggage, but was also in possession of a teddy bear from which he was never parted, and which accompanied him on all journeys. Michael's teddy bear was no ordinary creature, but was dressed like an admiral, complete with admiral's cap, and was secured to its loving owner by means of a piece of string attached to his wrist. I imagine I must have totally accepted this piece of eccentricity because I don't recall that it bothered me unduly, and certainly Michael was in no way embarrassed by his uniformed appendage, but we must have been the recipients of some strange looks from the other passengers on London tube trains as we made our way across the capital. In those wartime days we probably looked like a couple of evacuees, and I'm sure nothing about our

With my twin brother Tony (right) at Dawlish, 1937.

Family picnic at Lusley, Dartmoor. Father and mother on extreme left and various relations, 1936.

At Sidmouth in 1935 with our father's family.

With my first partner, Jean Prokter, at Dawlish, 1935.

Flying high at the Cone-Ripman School, 1942.

appearance suggested that we were pupils at one of the country's foremost stage schools. It was my duty to see that Michael was safely deposited at Taunton station, where his mother met him, and I would proceed alone to Devon.

I started working seriously for my dancing examinations while at Loddington Hall, and well remember travelling to Leicester for my RAD Elementary exam. It was a freezing winter, with snow and ice everywhere, and we were bitterly cold, a situation not helped by the fact that we had to set off quite early in the morning to reach Leicester by mid-day. They were not ideal conditions for a dancing exam, and we all tried to warm up in front of an inadequate electric fire in a bleak ante-room while we waited our turn to go in and perform, shivering not only from nerves, but from a temperature hovering around zero.

It was while I was doing my examinations in Leicester that I first met Dame Adeline Genée, who was one of the examiners. We grew accustomed to the idiosyncrasies of the various examiners and became adept at knowing exactly what each one was going to look for in our work.

'Oh, it's *her*!' we would say with dismay as we recognised a perennial Tartar, and we would know in a minute that she would be watching for arms, or beats, or whatever she was known to pounce upon. The examination scene became very familiar. While I was at Loddington Hall between the ages of ten and thirteen I took the RAD Elementary, Intermediate, Advanced, Solo Seal and Gold Medal. I have since been on the committee and judged examinations myself, so I know very well what the candidates are going through! When I was a student it was possible for a particularly talented dancer to take all the examinations at six-monthly intervals. Today there is an age limit which governs the entrants, although exceptions are made, and this is an improvement upon an earlier edict which made pupils wait a year between one examination and the next, a system which held back those who were especially gifted.

Russia looks upon its young potential dancers very differently, and has a more encouraging attitude towards all the arts, but here in the west we still have to break down a lot of barriers as far as theatre schools are concerned, and training for any artistic career. Fortunately, things are changing gradually, and Dance is now on the curriculum of many schools where once it was almost unheard of. It is sad that in this country the arts are always the first to suffer in any recession or financial crisis.

The fascinating thing about being a dancer is that there are no language barriers, and consequently one can go anywhere in the world and communicate. Through my art I have been able to meet royalty, great leaders of state, rich and poor in all continents of the world, the common tongue being the ballet. As I continue to travel, often retracing my steps to countries visited years ago, I find to my delight old friends everywhere. So much can be learned about foreign countries simply by studying their arts and cultures. By doing so, and being able to communicate because of it, more love and goodwill is spread than is distributed by any politicians. Every form of art is part of the history of a nation, and it is something which goes on for ever until it is destroyed by Man, either by wilful neglect or forced obliteration.

Chapter Two

A wartime childhood was an extraordinary existence, full of dramas which we accepted as everyday occurrences. How difficult it must be for children of today to appreciate how we lived in a country under siege. Bombs were falling, Londoners went to bed every night on platforms in Underground stations, and mass evacuation schemes were sending children away from their parents to stay with people they had never met in their lives. It all seems like a distant dream, but I have a vivid recollection of returning to school with Michael after a holiday. Our train was stuck about ten miles out of Bristol because a blitz was in progress. From our seats in the compartment we watched the whole city go up in flames under the German bombs.

During one wartime holiday my brother and I were on the beach at Dawlish, knowing perfectly well we should not have been there. It was surrounded by barbed wire, which we successfully negotiated in order to go swimming. There was a big RAF station just outside Exeter, and constant air activity around the estuary. Tony and I were sitting idly watching three planes, thinking they were RAF aircraft returning to base. The Cornish Riviera Express was coming round the coast, and as the planes swooped and started to machine gun the train we realised they were German fighters! Instinctively we threw ourselves flat on the beach and hoped for the best, although I cannot remember feeling scared. All I recall is the rat-tat-tat of the gunfire, which missed us and missed the train, fortunately protected by the cliffs. We heard later that all three planes had been shot down. One came down on the beach at Torquay, one on the moors, and one out at sea.

I spent much of the war in London, throughout the 'buzz bombs'.

One weekend I was staying with Grace Cone in her flat in Portman Square, and I remember very well the noise of the guns going off in Hyde Park, and going down into the deep shelters in Portman

Square. At the Cone School we were all led down into the basement when the air raid sirens went, but I think the only time I was ever really frightened was when we lived at Golders Green. My mother would come upstairs and grab us when we were fast asleep, and take us downstairs to the dubious sanctuary of the table shelter. The worst thing about the buzz bombs was the moment when the 'buzz' stopped, and there was nothing one could do but sit and wait for them to drop, one knew not where.

Both Tony and I had a musical education, and Tony started piano lessons when he was very young. We were both angelic looking choirboys at Dawlish Parish Church, and had piano lessons from the choirmaster, Nicholas Nepean, a fascinating man who had been High Judge of Northern Burma for many years and had retired to Dawlish. He was well into his seventies when we knew him, and made a tremendous impression on us both. I used to visit him during my summer holidays when I was at boarding school, but Tony, who was still at school in Dawlish, spent a lot more time with him than I. He lived in a beautiful house, full of Burmese and other oriental treasures. He also had a 'dumb piano' known as a clavioline. It had three octaves and could be made to play staccato or legato by turning a handle. Tony learned a great deal of music on that before he actually tried it out on a real piano.

I have always had a tremendous inquisitiveness. I wanted to know everything and question it, and I loved to listen to Mr Nepean's stories and anecdotes about his foreign travels as much as he loved to tell them.

There was the time when he was crossing the Indian Ocean in 1883, and the volcano Krakatoa erupted, covering his boat with ash; and the yarns about how he played his small, copper-lined piano to the Chindits, introducing them to Bach . . . . I mopped up all his stories like a sponge, with no idea that one day I too would travel the world and come back with a fund of stories. Whenever I have been to foreign countries I have always wanted to go everywhere and see all I could. My inherent restlessness would never allow me to stay two or three months in a country and not do anything. I was never bored – simply restless.

When on tour with Festival Ballet I served as a human atlas for the rest of the company. They would always ask me where we were, and what we were flying over at that particular moment, and I would know instinctively which mountain was below us. Right now, at this minute, I would love to get on a boat and sail up the Amazon, which is something I have always wanted to do. At heart I am an explorer – not only of places, but of people and information. My mind is full of snippets of both useful and useless facts collected over the years simply because of my insatiable curiosity or because something impressed me. Mr Nepean, for example, taught Tony and me all about curry, which he cooked to perfection. Once a week when I was at home we used to go to dinner with him and partake of his fabulous curries, the eating of which was almost a religious ritual. The spicy hotness burned our mouths with exquisite pain.

'Whenever you eat these hot curries,' advised Mr Nepean, as he watched the perspiration begin to stand out on our faces, 'you must always have plain sliced tomatoes as a side dish. When the curry gets too hot, just eat tomatoes.'

That is just one of those extraordinary nuggets of information stored up from childhood, and it immediately conjures up infallible memories of the person who imparted it.

In 1942 Mr Nepean took us on an outing to Praa Sands in Cornwall, not far from The Lizard. It was the first time I had been to that part of Cornwall, which I found unbelievably beautiful. We were almost at the end of The Lizard when we spotted a tanker going up the Channel about three miles out. As we watched there was suddenly the most tremendous explosion. The ship blew up in front of our eyes, probably having struck a mine. It seemed unreal, like watching a film.

Because we were not so aware of wartime dangers as adults were, we occasionally did ridiculous things. Tony and one of his friends built a canoe, which we sailed round to the coves near Dawlish, camping there overnight, much to our mother's consternation. We were nothing if not adventurous, but I can see now why the grown-ups thought we were simply foolhardy and not entirely to be trusted out of sight.

Above all, I think the thing for which I am most grateful to Nicholas Nepean is the fact that he instilled into both of us so much musical knowledge. Tony became extremely accomplished. In addition to playing the piano well, he also became a competent church organist when he was quite young. Because I have always loved music I found it easy to be a 'musical' dancer, and have always been amazed at the number of technically good dancers who are not in the least musical; they seem unaware of its demands on stage in the context of a ballet, and I find this hard to understand.

I had a very good piano teacher at Loddington Hall. She was a Frenchwoman who was perhaps too easy-going with me. Nobody needed to drive me to dance well, but the piano was another matter. I have never been good at sight-reading, probably because I have never afforded it the necessary concentration, but I could sit down and learn a piece of music. I would often put my own notes to it because I was fortunate enough to have a natural ear, so the end product always sounded quite satisfactory. When I went for my next piano lesson I would launch into my new piece, full of confidence that I knew it perfectly, but my self-satisfaction was invariably short-lived. At the end of my rendering there would be a brief silence, followed by the inevitable criticism.

'Yes, that's beautifully played, John, but it is not the right notes!'

My face would fall. I was sure I had done so well.

'It sounds exactly like the composer's music, but it is not correct,' my teacher would comment. 'Now you must go and learn it properly.'

Eventually the good lady had a nervous breakdown, but I like to think it had nothing to do with me.

I did not have problems of that kind with my dancing, and the first great acçolade I received, at a very early age, was the Adeline Genée Gold Medal. This is the highest award of the Royal Academy of Dancing, of which Genée was President. I was thirteen years old, and the youngest ballet student ever to win it – a fact which almost prevented me from winning it at all!

I was still at Loddington Hall, and had to make a trip to London for the event, to the Westminster Theatre, where I and the other contestants had to perform before an august panel of nine judges. They represented a formidable array of experts on dance, and included Adeline Genée herself, Ninette de Valois, Marie Rambert, Ruth French and Phyllis Bedells. The syllabus for the award covered every aspect of ballet. There was a set classical dance, and a demi-character dance which we had to choreograph ourselves. For some reason I had chosen the somewhat morbid theme of a man who was imprisoned and trying to get out – almost like *Petrouchka*. I rehearsed this piece religiously every evening at Loddington Hall in preparation for the great event.

The Adeline Genée awards were instigated in 1934 and were a series of medals – three for boys and three for girls – gold, silver, and bronze in each case. If the standards are not high enough then no award is made. When I entered there had been no male winner of the Gold Medal since 1937, so when I competed in 1943 the stakes were high. I therefore felt it a tremendous honour when the coveted award came to me. Little did I know at the time that one member of the panel who was later to have such an influence on my life had actually voted against me because of my age. Apparently she thought that thirteen was far too young an age for any recipient.

If I had not become a dancer I think I would have liked to be a marvellous pianist, despite my difficulties in playing the composer's notes! But I would have had to be somebody of the stature of Horowitz because of my streak of perfectionism. I can never make do with anything less than the best, and if for some reason I have to do so, then I feel totally dissatisfied and frustrated.

I can still fiddle around on a piano and produce fairly acceptable sounds; I suppose I might even play quite well if I put my mind to it. But that is something I must leave until later, rather as Dame Marie Rambert did. She is now ninety-four, and always wanted to play the piano well. Twelve years ago she decided she would do just that, so she set about learning to play in earnest. She can now play the most complicated Bach pieces incredibly well.

Some time ago I went to her home in Camden Hill to escort her to the Royal Festival Hall where she was to give a lecture with Anton Dolin and Ninette de Valois at the end of the Stravinsky Festival. When I arrived at her house she said, 'Come into the living room, John. Just before we go I must play you this piece. It is the most beautiful Bach Partita.'

So saying, she proceeded to sit down at the piano and rattle off the difficult piece of Bach. It is just another aspect of the extraordinary Marie Rambert, who was responsible for so much of my development in the world of dance. Another of her many facets is that she can recite all the Shakespeare sonnets by heart, which is an amazing feat of memory. The root of it all would apear to be self-discipline, which she has in abundance. It is not the easiest of attributes to acquire, and far more difficult to achieve than a discipline exerted from outside and imposed upon us.

Looking back at Loddington Hall days, I realise that although our dancing was extremely disciplined, both socially and academically it was lax, but as it was wartime this must have been true of many schools. We were virtually cut off from the outside world and left to our own devices in the magnificent grounds surrounding the great house.

The nearby town of Oakham was out of bounds, but because of the attraction of the boys' public school there, the lure of new male blood proved too much of a temptation for some of our more nubile students, and a few of the girls used to find their way to Oakham at weekends. Three girls were cycling back one afternoon when there was a tragedy on the very steep hill between Oakham and East Norton. Some of us had been out and we arrived back at school to be met by an air of silence and deep gloom, which pervaded the whole building. The brakes had failed on a girl's cycle while she was coming down the hill. She had gone over the handlebars, struck her head, and been killed outright. It was a great shock for us all. At that age it is very difficult to accept that one's contemporaries can actually die; there is something unreal about it because in the world of the young, only old people die. Suddenly our whole lovely carefree world had gone wrong with the intervention of death.

As a result of the accident, which had shaken everybody to the core, the privilege of having bicycles was withdrawn, quite understandably, but before that happened I had a bicycle problem of my own in the hilly terrain surrounding the school. There was a steep hill outside, and at the bottom was a farmyard and a sharp bend round to the school gates. I was cycling back from the village one weekend with some of my friends and was going so fast that I could not control the bike. The only way I could stop was to turn into the farm stackyard where there was an enormous heap of manure. Faced with the split-second decision of whether to go into the dung heap or the farmhouse wall, I chose the heap and headed straight for it. In I went, head first, leaving the saddle and landing smack in the middle of the pungent pile I had chosen in preference to the brick wall.

Covered from head to foot in the smelliest of effluent, I emerged from the heap, picked up my dung-encrusted bicycle and crawled back to school, where I was promptly grabbed by the Matron, who for once did not seem to be terribly pleased to see me. Amid a tirade of concern, abuse and distaste she tore my stinking garments from me, held them at arm's length, and almost hurled me bodily into a bath.

I never set out to be bad, nor was I a delinquent in any way. Most of the time I stayed out of trouble, but it again came my way when I successfully reduced an ancient tree to a pile of ashes. I was not deliberately destructive, but there was nothing I liked better than lighting fires and cooking things in the great outdoors. Perhaps there lurked within me a frustrated Boy Scout, or maybe it was all part of a sense of adventure. With two friends I had a most satisfying camp fire going one afternoon within the immediate precincts of an old yew tree at the side of the front lawn at school. The tree was fully sixty or seventy feet high, so was probably as old as the house itself.

We had a great time with our camp fire cookery, and went back indoors at the end of the day, completely unaware that we had failed to extinguish the fire so that there was no chance of it re-igniting. Perhaps a mischievous wind sprang up, or perhaps the gods who punish small boys for incendiarism were on duty that night. Whatever the reason, some hours later fire engines suddenly materialised and the front lawn was illuminated by a hideous red glow. Peering out of a window I realised to my horror that the excitement and conflagration centred on the hitherto magnificent yew tree in whose hospitable shadow we had spent the afternoon.

Retribution followed swiftly, and I was fined three weeks' pocket money, which was total catastrophe at that time because I was unable to purchase my weekly sweet ration – a luxury in those days of wartime austerity!

I loved trees, but somehow always seemed to set fire to them. Outside Dawlish was one of our favourite wild playgrounds, where the river ran through. During school holidays we would make our way there and catch tadpoles and minows. There was a very long, big old hollow log there, and I thought it would be an excellent idea to build a fire in it and cook some food, which we did. We were quite sure we had put out the fire before we left, but alas we had not, and it was a cue for the local fire brigade to turn out and do its stuff. Even Devonshire was not safe from my fire-raising.

My brother's experience of trees was not in this context, but he had the misfortune to fall out of one. It could have been disastrous, but fortunately he got caught up with one of the branches as gravity took its toll, and that prevented him from having a very unpleasant accident. We were always in scrapes of one kind or another, and it would be hard to say which of us was the ringleader. As far as I recall we used to encourage each other.

A lake in Loddington Hall grounds was the scene of another childish adventure which could have had serious repercussions. Some local boys had built a raft, which presented the most marvellous possibilities. The lake seemed harmless enough, and I often ferried the raft across its apparently untroubled surface, never thinking of the depth of the water beneath. The fun came to an abrupt end when one of the girls somehow fell from the raft. She couldn't swim, and had to be feverishly dragged out before she drowned. It was the cue for prompt action from those in charge, and the lake was henceforth declared out of bounds. Looking after us all must have been a nightmare, and it was doubtless a relief when we were returned to our parents at the end of term, sound in wind and limb.

Despite what would appear to be a life full of nothing but childish fun and games, we did work very hard at our dancing. The curriculum catered for normal school lessons during the morning and dancing occupied the afternoons. From the age of nine I was having one, or sometimes two ballet lessons a day, plus tap, national dancing, musical comedy and singing. It was intensive, and meant to be taken very seriously. Certainly for me there was nothing in the world more important. I had been given a wonderful opportunity to study and perfect the art for which I had been destined since the day I was born. Everything was falling into place; there was a natural automatic progression occurring. Schooldays were therefore much more than a day-to-day existence – they were a means to a whole way of life. Although I looked forward to going home for the holidays I never found school a hardship in any way.

Just before returning home for a holiday at the end of a summer term, a family of wild cats living in one of the Loddington Hall barns was blessed with a litter of kittens. They were beautiful little creatures, and I desperately wanted one to take home to Devonshire. I was determined to capture one, which was no easy feat because they scratched madly and had evaded me on several occasions. I kept trying, and eventually managed to get hold of one, which I put in a box and hid in my room until it was time to go home. At about the same time I imprudently completed a transaction with a boy in the village for some white mice. These too were destined for Devonshire at the end of term, and on the day of departure my luggage included two strange boxes – one containing a kitten and the other incarcerating a collection of white mice. It was an ill assorted mixture of travelling companions, especially bearing in mind the length of the journey between Rutland and Devon. I left school at about six in the morning, and after travelling all day the cat and mouse situation must have been fairly fraught, but the journey was completed without mishap to myself and my livestock.

My mother met me on Dawlish station platform, her pleasure at seeing me tempered by her dismay at my appearance. I always arrived home looking unbelievably scruffy. My hair was never cut during the term, my raincoat looked like an unmade bed, and on this occasion, clutched to my person, were two boxes which immediately excited my mother's curiosity.

'What have you got in those boxes?' she asked. Her voice sounded not only suspicious, but there were undertones of apprehension. I had a nasty feeling that she would be totally unprepared for an honest answer. I confessed to the kitten, but discretion forbade that I mention the mice at that stage of my arrival. That could all come later. There was something of a groan when I mentioned I had brought home a kitten, but it was given grudging sanctuary and then promptly disappeared, never to be seen again. I managed to smuggle the mice into the large garage at the back of the house, but I was never good at subterfuge and soon had to admit to their presence.

Mothers can be funny about mice, and mine did not seem to understand why I needed to import them into her well run household, but her dismay was short-lived because they too escaped and vanished. Perhaps somewhere in the neighbourhood was a very well fed kitten!

I found animals irresistible, and had what must have been a tiresome habit of collecting strays. The result was that whenever my parents moved house they were always encumbered by livestock in baskets and cages or on leads, because I would adopt animals and then have to go away on tour. This meant my parents had to take them over, and they were very long-suffering about my impulsive acquisition of various pets. Anton Dolin and I were in Norwich on tour with Festival Ballet when we came across a golden cocker spaniel tied up outside one of the shops. The poor thing had obviously been badly treated, so we bought it from its owner and took it home. For a time it stayed in our London apartment, but eventually, like all my pets, it ended up with my parents. Fortunately my father loved dogs, and was quite happy to take it. The spaniel became quite a character, and whenever I was at home he would come swimming with me. After going half a mile out in the sea I would suddenly feel his paws on my shoulder as he sought support because he was tired. He was also a great traveller, and discovered he could get on the morning bus to Dawlish, which passed the end of the garden. He would be away for some hours before boarding the afternoon bus back home!

Many things began to happen in 1942, and although dancing still played a major part in my life I began to do professional acting as a result of being sent for auditions from school. The war was omnipresent, and I recently discovered in an old scrap book a programme for an event which I had forgotten about, for one of the many wartime charities. It was a performance given by the Production Club at Toynbee Hall in aid of the Fund for Comforts for the Minesweepers. How quaint and unreal those wartime charities sound now, but at the time they were taken extremely seriously and were all desperately important. On that occasion I danced the man's solo from the *Swan Lake* Pas de Trois, and it is interesting to note from the programme that one of the three accompanists was Antony Hopkins. Two other dancers taking part were Annette Chappell, who went to Ballet Rambert, and David Davenport.

Having passed the Advanced examination of the Royal Academy of Dancing, and Solo Seal when I was twelve, I was unable to take my next examination until I was fourteen. This meant that although I kept up my dancing I was free to do other things. During 1942 I was chosen for a part in Vera Lynn's first film, *We'll Meet Again.* It was of course based on her famous song of the same title, and was full of wartime patriotism, as were most of the British films of that era. Vera Lynn was already well known as The Forces' Sweetheart. I remember her as being a genuinely nice person, very kind and unaffected. I have met her many times since then, and she is still unchanged, fame and Dame not having altered her in the least. Her voice seems to have grown in stature with the years, and today she is singing better than ever.

My first professional stage appearance came at the end of 1942 when I played Michael in *Peter Pan* at the Winter Garden Theatre, with Ann Todd as Peter and Joyce Redman as Wendy. I did the play again in 1943, this time with Glynis Johns as Peter and Alastair Sim giving a marvellous performance as Captain Hook.

Another film I took part in at that time was *They Were Sisters* with Phyllis Calvert, Anne Crawford, Dulcie Gray and James Mason, and the stars of the old Gainsborough days. We were on location at Godalming for about three weeks, and stayed at a lovely old hotel. A chaperone accompanied me and I had to do a certain amount of schooling while we were filming, but it was all great fun and no real hardship.

My father was invalided out of the navy in 1944, and early that year I played in *Crooked Sapling* by Charlotte Haldane with Norman Marshall's company at Cambridge Arts Theatre. Later that same year I got the part of Robin in Daphne du Maurier's play *The Years Between* at Wyndham's Theatre, with Nora Swinburne and Clive Brook. It ran for over a year, and then I went on tour with it, later doing the same role in the film with Michael Redgrave and Valerie Hobson.

It was very exciting to be in a West End play, and I was at Wyndham's at the time of VE Day, with all the sudden tumult of victory celebrations, the switching on of the lights and the dancing in the streets. There was a glamour about the theatre in those days which is somehow missing today. There are still glamorous people in the theatre, but it is a different world, and it is sad to see the passing of the really great days of the West End, with its sophistication and elegance . . . the polish of the Gingold-Kendall revues, and the successful British musical productions.

Nora Swinburne was always very kind to me, and was the first person to take me to The Ivy, that great theatrical restaurant, which left me goggle-eyed. I was overwhelmed to go in and see all those famous people who had just been names to me, and there they were, sitting all around me. Nora and I had a regular weekly treat, because in a street behind the Saville Theatre was a shop called Mario's, which made the most succulently marvellous cakes.

In those days of food rationing such luxuries were rare indeed, and how they were produced at that time I shall never know, but there they were – magnificent chocolate cakes, cream buns and exotic gateaux of all kinds lying in tempting array, and always before a Saturday matinée Nora and I would make the excursion to Mario's to buy our cakes.

I was suddenly in a world that for an ordinary schoolboy was unbelievable. It can be said, I suppose, that I was not an ordinary schoolboy because I was not at a traditional kind of school – I was at a stage school, but bearing in mind that I had not been brought up with a theatrical background, and our school was far removed from the West End and its theatres, I was extremely impressionable. There I was, meeting all the idols and famous movie stars of the time, and a little later, all the people in the dance world too. I did not see a great deal of ballet performances at that time because I was too involved with the acting side in theatre and films, but the names of famous dancers were magic. As far as ballet was concerned, my participation had still not happened professionally, but I was always quite adamant about what I wanted to be – a dancer, not an actor.

While I was at Wyndham's Theatre during the long run of *The Years Between*, Sadlers-Wells Ballet was at the New Theatre adjacent to Wyndham's, and I remember being very envious of 'the people next door' – dancers like Beryl Grey, Moira Shearer and Gillian Lynne, my old friend from Cone-Ripman. Because a lot of us knew each other we would laugh and joke with each other across the courtyard between the two theatres. Although I loved being in the play, how I longed to be on stage in the other theatre. I would often sit in my dressing room and wish I was dancing; it was a great sense of frustration.

If there was a Sadlers-Wells matinée on a day when I wasn't working I would always go and see the performance. One of the events I remember clearly was Svetlana Beriosova's first *Swan Lake*. It was a period of great creative activity in British ballet. All the Helpmann works were being done at the time, such as *Hamlet* and *Miracle in the Gorbals*. But for me it was still a world away; I was too young even to think of joining a ballet company. My lack of height was at that time a considerable worry to me. It was because I was an inch too short that I lost the part of Pip in the film *Great Expectations*. I did the screen test with Jean Simmons, who was at that time at the Aida Foster Stage School. We played the marvellous scene with Miss Havisham and the cobwebs, with Martita Hunt, but in the end the part went to Anthony Wager. I did not start adding to my height until I went to Australia with Ballet Rambert, and was terrified that I was not going to be tall enough to be a dancer.

Meanwhile I was also doing radio work, and took part in John Masefield's *Box of Delights* on Children's Hour, and *The Little Stuarts*, a play about the children of Charles I in which I played Prince James, later James II. But life was not all acting, and it was a dancing occasion when I was first brought into contact with Noël Coward. I was fifteen years old and taking part in a charity gala at Grosvenor House in aid of the Anglo-Polish Air Force. I had to dance a Polish Mazurka, and was terribly worried about the hat I had to wear. My father's sound advice was, 'If you find you can't manage the hat, throw it away.' During the dance I remembered his suggestion and did just that – which brought the house down! After the show Noël Coward, who had been in the audience, went up to my mother.

'Is that your son?' he asked, in those familiar clipped tones.

'Yes,' she replied, somewhat nervously.

'Don't let him get spoilt,' he instructed.

Then he turned to me and said, 'I expect to hear more of you, young man.'

That was the extent of our first meeting, but years later he was to create his only ballet for me, and for Festival Ballet. At the time of my encounter with him in 1945 I was facing a crossroads in my juvenile career. I had auditioned for the title role in Terence Rattigan's play *The Winslow Boy* and had been fortunate enough to get the part. At about the same time Marie Rambert approached me with an invitation to join her company, so I was suddenly forced to make a decision. Did I carry on acting for the time being, having been successful in getting a major West End role in a play which would obviously have a long run, or did I turn my back on acting and take up the chance of joining one of the country's major ballet companies? Deep down, I knew what I had to do, and that was to start dancing professionally. There was no question as to where my heart lay, although I did not want to let Rattigan down. Unfortunately, that was exactly what I knew I must do. I felt guilty, and apprehensive of his reaction. He was, after all, a very important man of the theatre, and one did not discard his roles lightly. I also held him in great personal regard.

When I summoned the courage to tell him of my decision he was very understanding. 'Of course you must go, John,' he said. 'Much as I would love to have you in this part, dancing is your life, and this decision has got to be.'

One of our most brilliant playwrights, Rattigan was also a wonderful man. He suffered for many years with leukaemia, periods of remission alternating with times of terrible pain. His death in 1978 saddened me very much.

The way through life is littered with friendships which dissipate for no other reason than that one has neither time nor opportunity to sustain them, but they remain as landmarks which have formed some kind of link and guidance, and for me Terence Rattigan's was such a friendship. After I went to Australia in 1947, where I remained for two years, our paths rarely crossed, except to meet at the theatre occasionally. I was abroad when he died and could not attend his memorial service, and I often greatly regret I did not endeavour to maintain contact with him in later years. I realise now how much he taught me, and how much I absorbed from him when I was an impressionable teenager. He would often take me to the theatre during his heyday of being our greatest West End playwright during the 1940s, and he represented to me everything a successful playwright should be. His lifestyle was very grand – a Rolls Royce and a beautiful house in Chester Square, and always a tremendous flair and elegance in his demeanour.

He loved cricket, which I did not much care for, but he also loved to go to Wimbledon, and as a fifteen-year-old I had never been. For my birthday that year he took me to his tailor in Savile Row and had the most beautiful suit made for me. I had never owned a suit of such

(Right) Antony Tudor's *Gala Performance,* Ballet Rambert, 1947. Left to right: Annette Chappell, Sara Luzita, Brenda Hamlyn, me, and company.

(Below) Ballet Rambert tour of Australia and New Zealand, 1947-49. Marie Rambert (in white hat), and our hosts (centre) with, l to r: Sally Gilmour, Walter Gore, Joyce Graeme, Paula Hinton, Vassilie Trunoff, Sara Luzita, myself and Brenda Hamlyn.

(*Right*) As The Rabbit Catcher in Andrée Howard's ballet *The Sailor's Return* with Ballet Rambert at Sadlers-Wells Theatre, 1947.

(*Below*) Ballet Rambert, 1947. With Annette Chappell in the Peasant *Pas de Deux* in *Giselle*.

quality and was immensely proud of it, feeling supremely elegant when I wore it in his company at the opening of Wimbledon. Almost unconsciously I learned from Terence so much about the theatre and the way to behave. At the time I was growing up I always sensed an aura about theatre people, which I still find when watching great actors at work, but somehow today it does not seem quite the same, which may simply be one of the penalties of growing older. We are less easily impressed, but we also lose something of the spontaneous joy of encounters with people or new situations.

It is perhaps only now I realise how lucky I was when growing up to have been influenced by such people as Rattigan. I knew my decision to begin my dancing career at that stage was the right one, and so I accepted the invitation to join Ballet Rambert. I joined as a soloist at the age of fifteen, without even an audition. I was to remain with the company for the next five years.

Chapter Three

It has been said before that if Dolin was my balletic father then certainly Marie Rambert was my balletic mother. The influence of both was immense.

I arrived at the Mercury Theatre, fresh from films and the West End, to join Ballet Rambert at a salary of six pounds a week. But I didn't care about the money because this was the beginning of my chosen profession. In that famous little theatre and its rehearsal room, the nursery of so many great dancers, choreographers and ballets, I began what was to be the rest of my life. It was a wonderful beginning and an excellent training ground – slogging away at the barre, learning roles quickly and being pushed on at a moment's notice, dancing eight times a week, touring constantly, looking for digs,and generally learning what a dancer's life was all about. And behind us all the time was 'Mim', screaming, shouting and cajoling.

My very first performance with Ballet Rambert was at the Theatre Royal, Brighton, on 5th November 1945. I danced the Scotch Dance from *Façade* with Paula Hinton and Jean Stokes. All the way down to Brighton in the train I kept going through the steps in my mind because I was so terrified that I would forget it or do something wrong. Fortunately nothing went amiss, and in the same programme I also got through the Tyrolean Dance from *Soirée Musicale* without any crisis. My dancing career was launched, and it was a wonderful feeling.

I was fortunate to have joined the company in its great days, and at first was awe-struck at working with people whose names I had only read about in ballet books. I joined at the same time as Paula Hinton and Belinda Wright, with whom I was later to have such a successful partnership. One had to be prepared for anything with Rambert. It could be corps de ballet work at one performance and a leading role at the next.

The repertoire was wide, and in addition to the classics we did all the early Ashton and Tudor ballets, with the advantage of having artists like Sally Gilmour, Walter Gore and Frank Staff. The unpredictable Mim Rambert could be difficult. She was strict and demanding, but if she shouted and scolded it was because she was interested. She was perhaps not the greatest of teachers, but she had the capacity and insight to see the potential in a young dancer and drag it out. She did just that with Sally Gilmour, whose talent lay in dramatic roles rather than as a classical dancer. She did not have a brilliant technique, but she was an incredible artist, as was shown in her great performances in *Lady Into Fox*, *Dark Elegies* and *Lilac Garden*. One thing I recall about Sally Gilmour was her phenomenal memory for ballets. Mention any ballet in the repertoire and she could remember not only her part, but everyone else's as well.

As she did with Gilmour, Rambert brought out all the natural qualities in her dancers, and being in her company comprised a very formative period in my life. There was such a sense of ballet history and tradition with Rambert, going back to the Diaghilev days when she, as a pupil of Jacques Dalcroze who initiated 'Eurythmics', was called in by Diaghilev to count for Nijinsky during rehearsals for *Rite of Spring*. Rambert's teachers had included Cecchetti and Astafieva, the great teacher from St Petersburg, so I was on the receiving end of enormous experience. Shortly after I joined the company I heard that Rambert, who was among the adjudicators when I entered for the Adeline Genée Gold Medal two years previously, had voted against my having it because she thought I was too young! Yet there I was at the age of fifteen as a soloist with her company.

It was by no means an easy life. We were all worked very hard, often to the point of exhaustion, but we loved it all, and despite our grumbles, we loved Rambert. She was full of temperament and kept her finger on the company pulse in unconventional and disconcerting ways, one of these being that she would scream at dancers from the wings in the middle of a performance. One would be preparing for a pirouette in front of a full house of what one hoped were admiring patrons, and suddenly from the wings would come Rambert's stentorian tones, 'Pull up! Straighten that leg!' It was all enough to make one totter uncertainly and mess up the whole thing. Sometimes I'm sure the audience heard every word.

Frank Staff was one of the company who refused to be intimidated, and we were always very amused at his stands against Mim's authoritarianism. Her classes were always extremely hard, often I thought, unnecessarily so, and they were made difficult just because she felt they had to be. All the time we were at the barre the little upright figure in blouse and trousers would walk around, going from one dancer to another. One would sense her presence if she was creeping up from behind. Then suddenly her hand would chop sharply between one's shoulder blades.

'Crack a nut!' she would snap demandingly, often really hurting as she made her attacks from the rear.

Down and back went the shoulders instantly under the onslaught while we outwardly stung and inwardly seethed, but the action always had the desired effect. One day in class she crept up behind Frank Staff, who must have been in rebellious mood, and decided he had had quite enough of Rambert's provocative nonsense for one day.

The small figure strutted up behind Frank as he stood at the barre.

'Crack a nut!' she shouted, chopping him smartly between the shoulder blades. At this point Frank promptly and deliberately fell flat on his face, feigning great indignation at being knocked over.

The tours were particularly demanding, often lasting as long as fourteen weeks, and taking us up and down the British Isles, from the south coast up to Kendal, Wick and Inverness. My mother came with the company on my first tour because it was thought I still needed looking after at the tender age of sixteen, having been thrown into a new strange world of travelling, theatres, and ever-changing digs. I have said previously she was never a typical Ballet Mother, and this was perfectly true. She never set out to interfere with my training in any way, and even on that first tour she kept very much in the background, but I was well aware that she was inwardly furious because she thought I was being grossly over-worked. This was all part of Rambert's hard training ground.

There was little relaxation, and I seemed to be dancing all the time. Often I would dance three ballets in one evening. In a typical programme I might start with the Pas de Trois from *Swan Lake,* go on again to dance *Spectre de la Rose* and finish up the evening with *Gala Performance.* One particular evening towards the end of that tour stands out in my mind. We were at the Arts Theatre, Cambridge. It was the usual hectic evening for me, and I was in three ballets. Ihad already danced the Pas de Trois, followed by *Spectre* and still had the last ballet to get through. Having been dancing eight performances a week I must have been extremely tired – more than I realised. When I made my grand exit in *Spectre*, jumping out through the window, I collapsed in the wings, quite unable to get up again.

To my amazement, my quiet and gentle mother, who happened to be standing next to Marie Rambert, suddenly exploded with untypical vehemence. She turned to Rambert and shouted indignantly, 'You're killing my son! You're killing him!'

Rambert was quite unruffled by this unexpected outburst. 'Don't worry, Mrs Gilpin,' she murmured soothingly. 'Please don't worry. It is very good experience for him. It will give him stamina.'

Spectre has always been a terrifying ballet to dance really well. It depends so much on atmosphere, and is not, as is often thought, just a fireworks piece for the male dancer, although for him it is ten minutes of non-stop dancing. I first danced the role with Sally Gilmour when I was sixteen, and because it was Nijinsky's most famous role it is inevitable that any dancer who attempts it will be compared with him, even though today's critics never saw Nijinsky. The result was that the newspapers seized upon the comparison, and underneath a headline proclaiming: 'SIXTEEN-YEAR-OLD IN NIJINSKY ROLE', went on to say: 'If this lad is not over-tried in his formative period he seems likely to go very far indeed.' Perhaps the critic was issuing a friendly overt warning to Marie Rambert not to wear me out, which I am sure must have pleased my mother! But Rambert was not noted for the soft approach. Who knows, perhaps it really did give me stamina?

Over the years I have learned so much about *Spectre* during the hundreds of times I have danced it, and much later in my career I had the experience of working on it with Tamara Karsavina, the ballerina who first danced it with Nijinsky. I felt honoured that I was able to go a long way towards getting back to the original form by receiving tuition from the great man's partner.

It is a ballet with which I felt a great affinity, and there was a direct line of tuition extending back to the great Nijinsky himself. I learned the role from William Chappell, who was taught by Anton Dolin, who in turn learned it from Nijinsky's understudy, Nicholas Zverev. Wherever Nijinsky danced, audiences always wanted to see him in *Spectre*, because of his amazing elevation and his legendary ability to appear to 'hover' during the leaps. As it was impossible for him to dance the role as often as requested, Sverev used to dance in his place sometimes at matinées.

Despite the hard work with Rambert there were lighter moments. On looking back, some incidents seem hilariously funny, but at the time they were major disasters.

In *The Fugitive,* a dramatic Andrée Howard ballet, the girls all wore beautiful ball gowns with amazing shirts made of yards and yards of material. We had to dance a tango in which I partnered Barbara Grimes, daughter of Grimes, the famous cartoonist. We were in a line across the stage during the ballroom scene, with our partners in front of us, and we had to lift them. All the girls went up gracefully, but I must have leaned a little too far back and could not control the lift. To my great horror I felt myself going further and further back, like a slow motion film. There was not a thing I could do about it, and I collapsed on the floor. Barbara's dress was so voluminous that it covered both me and my error of judgement. I groped my way around under the yards of tulle which formed her skirt and got to my feet as rapidly as possible with the amazing result that only those on stage were aware of my fall.

Another near tragedy came during a performance of *Simple Symphony* in which I had taken over Walter Gore's part. I was partnering Sally Gilmour when to my terror I felt my trouser zip give way. I was panic-stricken. I realised I had to get through the rest of the pas de deux holding not only my partner, but also my trousers. I clutched at them wildly, still trying to support Sally, and managed to tuck the top into my dance belt with the fervent hope that they would remain anchored for the duration of the performance, especially when I had to do the lifts. Providentially they defied the laws of gravity and I was spared the embarrassment of trousers round my ankles, but my nerves were shattered.

Belinda Wright was not so fortunate when I partnered her in a memorable performance of *Spectre de la Rose*. She was sitting in the famous chair, and when she got up to dance her frilled petticoat slid gently down to her feet. With great presence of mind she gracefully stepped out of it and carried on, but that was not the end of the mishaps. While I was whizzing around the stage I had kicked the rose under the chair, and it wasn't there for her to pick up – an essential part of the action. By this time Belinda was a quivering wreck, but went on undaunted, trying desperately to ignore Marie Rambert, who was groping around from the wings with a walking stick, trying to hook the petticoat. Out of the corner of our eyes we saw the dreaded garment slide off the stage on the end of the stick, in full view of the audience! Belinda was sure that night must be the end of her career, and had never felt so mortified. Needless to say, she fully recovered and went on to greater things.

Joyce Graeme incurred Rambert's displeasure when we were at Stratford-on-Avon. We were standing around on stage, relaxing and smoking, waiting for Rambert to start rehearsal. She duly arrived, and Joyce left her cigarette on top of a stool at the side of the stage. A few minutes later came a terrible scream as Rambert, without looking, sat on the stool from which she rose rapidly, noisily, and painfully. Joyce was in the doghouse for some time after that episode.

While we were at Sadlers-Wells Theatre in 1947 there was a great event happening in the hallowed realms of Covent Garden. Ballet Theatre descended from America and had London's ballet audiences at its feet. The excitement was tremendous – ballets we had never seen, dancers we had only read about, and a great transatlantic fervour permeating the whole occasion. Rambert's dancers and the Americans were dashing to and fro to see each other's performances, and it was a truly exciting period, being able to see all those great dancers – Jerome Robbins, Michael Kidd, Nora Kaye, Alicia Alonso, John Kriza and André Eglevsky. For me as for many others it was a new awakening in the dance world of Great Britain. After the wartime austerity of the London theatre, even allowing for the Trojan work done by our own companies, here was something new, glamorous, and sensational. It was a glorious summer for London's balletomanes, and they took Ballet Theatre to their hearts.

In 1947 Ballet Rambert embarked upon what turned out to be almost a world tour. I was just seventeen, and the family was against letting me go, but I managed to persuade them. Because I was so young I had to have a legal guardian before I was allowed to leave the country, so for the purposes of the tour I was 'adopted' by the Rambert Manager, John Dowey. My father and Mr Dowey had to appear before Bow Street magistrates before a licence could be granted. It was at first intended that the tour would be for six months, but it turned out to be sixteen, three spent in New Zealand. We had the honour of being the first British ballet company to visit Australia after the war.

We embarked for the Antipodes with a repertoire of thirty-two ballets and a company of thirty-six dancers, including such experienced artists as Sally Gilmour, Paula Hinton, Walter Gore, Frank Staff, Elizabeth Schooling and many others, plus myself and my contemporary, Belinda Wright.

At the time we left there were no ships going via Suez, so we went on the *Aquitania* from Southampton to Halifax, Nova Scotia, and flew from there to San Francisco, where we had to wait for two weeks. It was an exciting place in which to wait,and we found that no hardship at all. The boat trip was an amazing experience, and I well remember seeing white bread for the first time since the war, being able to eat all the sweets one wanted, and the luxury of real butter after the long years of rationing. From San Francisco we went the rest of the way on the liberty boat *Marine Phoenix*, on which we slept in bunks used by the American Marines, because the ship was just as they had left it. We could not have cared less about anything; it was all a great adventure. On we went to Samoa, then to Fiji, Auckland and Sydney, the trip taking three weeks to complete. It was, however, not entirely pleasure, and we had to have a mind to the fact that we were dancers, so we did barres every day and exercised to keep ourselves in trim.

We arrived at last in Australia, and opened at the Prince's Theatre in Melbourne in November, where the Australians gave us a tremendous welcome. We were inundated with goodwill and hospitality, thoroughly enjoying our first experience of being feted, both on stage and off. We played in Melbourne for two months and sold out every performance. They seemed to love everything in our repertoire, which included the early Anthony Tudor ballets, some by Andrée Howard, and some works by Frederick Ashton.

It was a triumph, not only for we who were dancing, but for Marie Rambert in particular. She was the undoubted star of the whole trip, and always on last nights, wherever we were in the big cities, she would make her curtain speech and then, to the delight of the audiences, she would perform her famous cartwheels right across the stage.

What had not been realised when we got to the Melbourne theatre was that this star would require a star's dressing room, and the best room had been allotted to Paula Hinton and Joyce Graeme. Rambert thought she should have the best quarters, and announced this in no uncertain terms. Paula and Joyce did not feel inclined to move out, their case being that as Rambert was not actually dancing she did not require a dressing room – and certainly not the best one. But Rambert had her own means of dealing with this situation, and in the midst of all the arguments and discussions we heard Paula talking to Rambert behind some flats backstage. Eventually Paula emerged, hysterical with laughter, and bade us creep round and look at the unparalleled performance in progress behind the flats. Looming large in the action was a big metal dustbin, and there was Rambert with her head in it, moaning like a member of a traditional Greek chorus. When she realised we were there she stood up and surveyed us, eyes full of tears and her hair all down her face.

'This miserable company!' she cried in anguish. 'Nobody cares about me at all.'

It was impossible for anyone to be angry with her for long, and in the end the girls said, 'Oh all right, you can have the best room if you want it.'

As always, Rambert did things her way, and succeeded!

When I was eighteen I learned to drive, having my first lessons in an old Buick in the wilds of the Australian bush. I picked up the mechanics of driving very rapidly, and with the misplaced confidence of youth soon thought I was totally competent to drive anywhere. My inherent impatience got the better of me, and it was not long before I ventured into the Australian traffic with little heed to the absence of a valid driving licence. One never-to-be-forgotten Friday evening I was cruising over Sydney Bridge in the rush hour, full of bravado, power at my finger tips – marvellous! I drew up at the toll gate, stopped the car in approved fashion with great efficiency, and then to my horror discovered that I couldn't start it again. Meanwhile the rush hour traffic was building up menacingly behind me for what looked like miles. I began to panic, my earlier confidence by this time dissipating rapidly. Nothing I did to the wretched car made any difference, and it resolutely refused to start. I went through all the usual ritual of looking hopefully at the dashboard instruments and peering under the bonnet, with the traffic queue behind me growing irrevocably longer. I felt my face get redder and redder. Any minute somebody was going to be interested enough to ask to see my driving licence, and of course I didn't have one!

The toll gate attendant, by that time also becoming disturbed at the bottleneck on his doorstep, then proffered his assistance. After a brief survey of the hunk of machinery in my charge he stood up and announced, 'I'm not surprised it won't go. You haven't any petrol in it!'

'What can I do?' I wailed. 'Where do I get petrol in the middle of Sydney Bridge?' I took another desperate look at the traffic queue, which by this time had become like a nightmare. Fortunately the man in the car behind me produced a can of petrol, and shaking with relief I drove on my way, thankful not to be able to hear them tell the story of the stupid Pommy trying to drive without petrol.

Australian hospitality never faltered, and during one of our free weekends in Sydney we were taken up to the Blue Mountains. We went by train and were then met by our hosts with horses, and taken to a ranch in the foothills. We spent the rest of the weekend on horseback in beautiful wild country with very high mountains and picturesque lakes, where we had our first glimpse of the glamorous lyre birds and the kookaburras.

Madame Rambert rode in a suky, which was a horse-drawn buggy, and insisted that Belinda Wright and Sally Gilmour did the same.

'I'm not having my ballerinas riding on horseback,' she said firmly. Indeed, it was a fatal mistake for the rest of us to spend so much time in the saddle. When we arrived back in Sydney after the weekend we were painfully stiff, and had to dance the following night. I was dancing *Spectre* and was so sore and bruised that I could hardly move. It was a seemingly geriatric spectre who took the stage that night!

As tourists we saw more of Australia than most Australians. I had an apartment in Bondi for a time, and in Melbourne six or seven of us shared a house. We were there for the first Christmas away from home, and had seven Christmas cakes given to us. It was a novelty for us to spend Christmas Day on the beach instead of having the traditional English Christmas when one waits for the first snowfall.

We flew from Sydney to Auckland, New Zealand, by Sunderland flying boat, then toured the North and South Islands by train. While we were on the Sunderland an outboard engine fell out, which caused more than a little consternation among the company.

'Don't worry,' said the steward soothingly. 'We can always land on water even on three engines.'

Fortunately, I never worry about embarking on flights. If the time is ripe for me to die then I'll die, whether I am on a plane or not.

Australia presented a great experience. I could not have wished for a better opportunity to spread my wings, coming as it did when I was so young and at the beginning of my dancing career. I made many friends there and had the chance to establish a reputation outside my own country which, for a dancer not yet out of his teens, was rare indeed. At the end of our strenuous tour we were all tired but elated at our obvious success. As for me, the enforced independence of being in a strange country thousands of miles from home had made me mature rapidly as nothing else could have done. Although the company was like a family, I was standing – and dancing – on my own two feet.

Chapter Four

We returned to London in February 1949 after a very exhausting five weeks at sea. It was a very cold early spring day when we arrived at Euston. My family was there to meet me, and didn't recognise me; they walked straight past me, as I had collected a deep sun tan and grown both taller and broader during those two years in Australia.

A lot of the company members stayed behind in Australia, some of them to get married. We were minus people like Joyce Graeme, Margaret Scott, Sally Gilmour and Rex Reid, and sadly Ballet Rambert as we knew it broke up when we came home. I had ideas of going to what was then Sadlers-Wells Ballet, but Roland Petit and the Ballets de Paris were in London that summer. Belinda Wright was already with the company, having come back from Australia earlier. I was delighted when Roland invited me to join his company, and I did so. So with such international stars as Colette Marchand, Renée (Zizi) Jeanmaire, Gordon Hamilton, Janine Charat and Milorad Miskovitch I began to dance for the second company to feature in my professional life.

In the meantime I had approached Ninette de Valois about joining Sadlers-Wells. It came as something of a surprise when she came up with the suggestion that I should then go and do my duty for king and country by doing my National Service. Such patriotic notions were all very well, but I could not see the point of giving two years of my life at that crucial stage of my training, at the age of nineteen. What a futile gesture it appeared to be, as the war had finished in 1945, and it was said that National Service was almost due to end anyway.

I had not been encouraged by my brother's experience of National Service. He had joined the RAF at the age of eighteen, and had spent the whole time up in the Orkneys! What would I do, I thought, if they stuck me in some outpost for the next two years? Having trained all my life to be a dancer it seemed the height of folly to give it all up at that point in order to spend a couple of years doing nothing to contribute either to my good or the military prestige of the British nation. But Ninette was adamant that I should go and 'do my bit', despite the fact that English male dancers were very scarce at that time. In any case, some of my contemporaries had gained exemption from National Service. Childishly, I thought it just wasn't fair. Had I joined Sadlers-Wells at that time my whole life and career would of course have been very different. But it is an ill wind . . . . and I joined Roland Petit's company instead, doing a tour with them, and eventually going to France, thus avoiding the necessity of exchanging ballet dancing for square-bashing for two years.

It was a very satisfying experience, and a great excitement to be a soloist in a more international company. There was also the added interest of being able to dance with Jeanmaire, and during our Paris season Margot Fonteyn came over as guest artist with the company. The whole group was more fraught with temperament than an English company, and there were countless rows in hotels because the French were terribly particular about their nourishment, always complaining about food and wine, and they had to have their steaks cooked to a point of perfection. During our four months in Paris I was amazed at the magnificence of the stars' dressing rooms. No expense was spared, and they would have them designed to their taste by some of the leading designers of the day. It was all a far cry from the scruffy dressing rooms endured by leading British dancers. There was comedy too, and while we were on tour in England we did a matinée for old age pensioners in Oldham which turned into a rout. Roland had created a humorous ballet, *Oeuf à la Coque*, all about the goings-on in a kitchen. In the last scene, the chickens, two of whom were danced by Jeanmaire and Marchand, attacked the chefs, of which I was one. That particular afternoon the company was bored, and we decided to send up the whole show, which started with the conductor coming in through the stalls in drag, and climbing into the orchestra pit complete with feathered hat. From that moment it went from bad to worse, culminating in a free for all, with onions and fruit being thrown at the elderly patrons, who seemed to have a whale of an afternoon.

When we came to London we opened with *Carmen* before Paris saw it. It was of course magnificent, with outstanding settings by Clavé, and Jeanmaire a revelation, partnered by Petit, creating a Carmen such as had never been seen before. We did a lot of new works with Petit, who was a great innovator, and his works were always regarded as a new departure in ballet, combining as they did the classical and the modern. I stayed with Ballets de Paris for a year, as a result learning how to speak French fluently.

Looking back over my career there is very little I regret, despite the many changes of fortune which inevitably beset any artist. If there must be a regret then it is that in all my twenty-two years with Festival Ballet we had to concentrate, for financial reasons, on the box office draws such as *Swan Lake*, *Nutcracker*, and the other classics, which became tedious. One of my great regrets is that I did not work with Sir Frederick Ashton as much as I would have wished. He is my favourite choreographer, and I think I was his kind of dancer – indeed, he has always told me so. One work he did re-create for me was *Vision of Marguerite*, a ballet I had done with Rambert in the early stages of my career, when it was called *Mephisto Valse* danced to the Liszt music. Ashton originally created this ballet for Markova in the 1930s. He remounted it for Festival Ballet with Markova and Dolin in mind, but as they were away in the United States I danced it with Belinda Wright and Oleg Briansky. It had its first performance in its new form at the Stoll Theatre on 3rd April 1952, Ashton having eliminated the corps de ballet from the new production. There were beautiful sets and costumes by James Bailey, and according to Julian Braunsweg in his book *Ballet Scandals*, Ashton's fee for mounting the work was £50. Braunsweg believed that for some reason Ashton was never paid!

One work created for me was Noël Coward's *London Morning*, but even *Witch Boy*, for which I was best known, was originally created in Holland for Norman McDowell. I feel therefore that at times I missed out creatively, and when *Witch Boy* was brought to the stage for Festival Ballet the critics were amazed to discover I had any versatility or dramatic ability. My main reputation as a dancer had until then always rested upon a virtuoso technique. I was always regarded as either a whirling Dervish or a beautifully mannered, plastic fairytale prince. The critics knew nothing of the dramatic actor bursting to get out, and unable to do so.

As I look back on reviews of the time it is interesting to note the number of times they refer to my apparent 'aloofness', my 'fixed expression' and 'strained smile'. I wanted to prove that I was much more than a charming prince, but chances were few and far between. Albrecht in *Giselle* gave some opportunity for acting ability and is one of the great roles, with more scope than Siegfried in *Swan Lake*. A lot can be done with Siegfried, but so many productions make it a very dull, stereotyped, partner role.

Many great opportunities came my way, so it would be ungracious to carp. I was able to build a reputation by dancing with ballerinas with whom I would never have had the chance to dance had I been at the Royal Ballet, although I later danced with many of their ballerinas too. I therefore have little cause for complaint.

While I was dancing with Roland Petit and his company, what was to become my major ballet company was having its birth pangs on the other side of the English Channel. Alicia Markova, Anton Dolin, and a corps de ballet recruited from the Cone-Ripman School gave a season at the Empress Hall in London, with a fit-up stage by Benn Toff, who later became Stage Director of Festival Ballet. The group also danced in large halls throughout the country where ballet had not previously been staged. Their first performance outside London was at the Town Hall, Newcastle-upon-Tyne on 12th September 1949.

My time with Roland Petit's company brought a widening of my ballet spectrum, and proved to be an enormously enjoyable experience.

Certain performances with Petit were memorable, and at least one was terrifying. One of the roles I danced with his company was that of The Dandy in *Le Beau Danube*. In the finale was a spectacular entrance in which I had to leap across the stage. I made my grand entry, and to my horror, tripped and fell. Fortunately, a split second reaction came to my aid and I was able to turn the trip into a complete head-over-heels, somehow coming up into an appallingly contrived position which brought a roar of good-natured and indulgent applause! Not a method of gaining audience approval which is to be recommended, but I was relieved it turned out as well as it did. Such accidents do happen from time to time, and one could write a whole book on ballet disasters. In *Nutcracker* I always performed a fast pirouette followed by a slow pirouette, and when I had achieved it I felt very pleased with myself. During one never-to-be-forgotten performance I did the first pirouette, which turned out beautifully, but the second time I slowed down to such an extent that I finished with my back to the audience! I quickly whipped round, but there is no fooling a Christmas audience well versed in *Nutcracker*. They spotted it immediately and roared with laughter, which served me right.

The Petit company was contracted to go to Hollywood to make a film, but I had no wish to go, and had been invited to join the Marquis de Cuevas company – a very big international company. Although I did many new ballets with Roland Petit, de Cuevas was a more classical company. I was anxious to start dancing the big roles, and this seemed to be the opportunity I was seeking.

With Le Grand Ballet de Marquis de Cuevas (to give its full title), I was able to dance the full *Swan Lake*. It was a chance to be in the company of such dancers as Tamara Toumanova, George Skibine, Marjorie Tallchief and Rosella Hightower. I duly joined de Cuevas and stayed with them for six months, during which John Taras put on a new ballet, *Persephone,* for Rosella Hightower and André Eglevsky, danced to Schumann's 'Spring Symphony.' Unhappily, just before the first performance Eglevsky tore a leg muscle, with the result that I had to learn the part and perform it in three days. I also found myself partnering Rosella Hightower in my very first 'Black Swan' pas de deux from *Swan Lake*, and the *Nutcracker* pas de deux. I had previously danced *Nutcracker* when I was with Rambert, but only the second act.

Eglevsky, who taught me 'Black Swan' had in turn learned it from Dolin – just another example of how ballet tradition is passed from one dancer to another down the generations. In a conversation with my old friend Peter Williams, former editor of *Dance and Dancers* and first press officer for Festival Ballet, he voiced a viewpoint I had not previously considered. It was that the position I held in British ballet from the time I joined Rambert meant I was one of the few male dancers whose dance heritage came down in direct line from Diaghilev and de Basil. I was therefore one of the few remaining links

(*Right*) Ballet Rambert; *Spectre de la Rose* with Sally Gilmour, 1946.

(*Below*) Ballet Rambert, 1946. With Sally Gilmour in Antony Tudor's ballet, *The Descent of Hebe.*

Ballet Rambert tour of Australia and New Zealand, 1947-49. Part of the company resting with the horses during a riding trip in the Blue Mountains, New South Wales.

With Belinda Wright during the week-end visit to the Blue Mountains, New South Wales.

in the chain descending from the historic days of the Russian ballet. Peter William's statement set me thinking, and I realised he was right. It is something which makes me proud, but at the same time very humble.

I had been taught by Marie Rambert, coached by Karsavina for *Spectre*, learned from, and worked with Alicia Markova and Anton Dolin, both of whom were with Diaghilev, and been privileged to partner former ballerinas from the de Basil company. Because of wartime restrictions on travel, plus the necessity of national service, the British male dancers of the forties had been more limited in their opportunities. Entering the ballet world as I did, immediately after the war, I happened to be in the right place at the right time to benefit from worldwide experience. What luck it was to be able to reap such a harvest of knowledge from travel as well as from the great names of the dance.

Through being with Roland Petit and the de Cuevas company I was able to come into contact with some of the important artists and choreographers, watching them create. To be dancing in front of backcloths designed by Salvador Dali and Picasso was an inspiration in itself, but then of course there were the dancers themselves. I remember volunteering for the corps de ballet in *Tricorne* while I was with de Cuevas, simply in order to be on stage with the great Leonide Massine. He joined the company to dance his original role of The Miller in his ballet, which he created in 1919. Toumanova danced the role of The Miller's Wife for de Cuevas. Just to share a stage with such dancers was very exciting, and watching Massine, the perfectionist at work was unforgettable.

It is sad today to meet young dancers who seem to be unaware of the great people of that generation, and of the history of the art they are studying, the profession they aspire to. I look back and ask myself how I knew about them, and I think the answer is that I listened and I read, devouring books, magazines – anything about ballet, and listening to conversations between teachers and dancers. Writers like Arnold Haskell and Cyril Beaumont contributed so much to the written history of the ballet. Do our young potential dancers still read similar books? I have often been amazed when I have mentioned to students such dancers as Sokolova and Lopokova and been met with a blank stare. The ballet as a profession is not just a question of learning to dance and having a great technique; there must also be an appreciation of the whole magic history of the ballet as an art.

Perhaps it is not a good idea to look back and compare 'then and now'. It is so easy to become pompous and boring by stating that things are not what they were; it must be a sign of middle-age . . . Yet I *am* going to say it: There are not the great personalities dancing today that there were thirty years ago. Markova, Dolin, Fonteyn, Beriosova, Nerina, Elvin, and Grey. It did seem to be a very progress of time. But who has replaced them? Internationally we have Nureyev and Baryshnikov, and one or two others, but I look back to the days when one could go to Covent Garden and see a galaxy in one evening. A performance of *Sleeping Beauty* could give us Fontey, Beriosova, Nerina, Elvin, and Grey. It did seem to be a very special era just after the war, or is my nostalgia leading me astray? The older generation says, 'You should have seen Pavlova.' Eventually they will say, 'You should have seen Markova' or Fonteyn. Not only is the grass always greener on the other side of the fence; it was always greener years ago!

When I joined de Cuevas Serge Golovine was one of the leading dancers, and had been for some time. He was dancing *Spectre de la Rose*, and then I also danced it. There was never any rivalry between Golovine and myself, but the audiences became partisan. He had his following, and I had mine from my days with Roland Petit, so there were always audience factions. There were those who came for the Gilpin *Spectre* and those who came for Golovine's.

At the end of six months with de Cuevas I was homesick and longing to get back to England. In all, I had been travelling the world for four years, and felt it was essential for me to go back home. I arrived at the very moment Julian Braunsweg, who had been touring Markova and Dolin's company, was enlarging it with a view to launching a full scale ballet company. As 'Stars of the Ballet' it opened at the Davis Theatre, Croydon on 20th March 1950, the programme consisting of solos, pas de deux, and corps dances. The tour was due to end in June at the Royal Albert Hall, but Markova unfortunately could not complete the season as she had to go into hospital for the removal of her appendix, so the beautiful Russian dancer Violetta Elvin stepped in.

Looking back, it seems an extraordinary fact of life that I never saw Anton Dolin dance until the days of Festival Ballet. I was still touring Australia with Rambert when he and Markova came back to London in 1948. I did not have the opportunity of meeting him until 1949, in Paris, where I was dancing with the Marquis de Cuevas company. It was an encounter which was the forerunner of a dramatic change in my career.

I was rehearsing one day with the company at the Salle Pleyel when Dolin suddenly came into the studio. The man was of course a legend in the dance world; everybody seemed to know him, everybody talked about him. I decided that I was not prepared to let him see I was either impressed or overawed by his presence. I had already been round the world, experienced the intoxication of homage and adulation, and was childishly conceited. I was a kind of ballet matinée idol, with immature good looks which were for a long while not to my advantage, and I foolishly thought I knew a lot already. Underneath all that insufferable bravado was my youthful insecurity and a certain shyness. I was still in awe of great dancers, and here was the world-famous Anton Dolin entering our rehearsal room.

'Where's Gilpin?' I heard him ask ballet master John Taras, who pointed to me across the room. I wondered why on earth he wanted me, and was startled to see him striding towards me. Dolin's powerful personality has been known to intimidate young dancers, with that dominant air and witty tongue which can sear as easily as it can blandish.

He stopped in front of me, and when he said, 'I have a message for you from Marie Rambert,' I smiled nervously and said nothing. 'She said that if I saw you,' Dolin went on, quite unperturbed by my lack of response, 'I was to give you a big kiss from her.'

He then proceeded to carry out Madame Rambert's instructions to the letter, relaying the affectionate kiss on my astonished mouth in full view of the assembled company. Not only was I embarrassed, but I was too petrified to make any reply or acknowledgement other than a flustered, muttered, 'Thank you.'

As a result he thought I was rather ill-mannered and that my reluctance to communicate depicted I was off-hand and conceited. It was not an auspicious beginning to our friendship and working partnership, which has now lasted for thirty-one years, through thick and thin. None of us is without fault, and for all his arrogance, false humility, showmanship and luck of the devil, there is also gentleness, generosity, and a tremendous loyalty. Of course there have been catastrophic moments during our long friendship. After all, he is a typical Leo, and astrologically my opposite zodiac sign, but perhaps I needed to absorb some of his energy and fire for my own character. I hope I have given some of the Aquarian qualities in return. Suffice to say that more than a quarter of a century has elapsed and we still remain great friends.

Anton Dolin's status in twentieth-century ballet is unique, and he was the first British *danseur noble*. I have always watched and learned all I could from him.

Six months after our unfortunate first meeting I was back in London. Dolin was in Paris looking for new dancers. He and Markova had been approached by Julian Braunsweg to form a new company. Although nobody knew it at the time, this was the company which was to become Festival Ballet. My former teachers, Grace Cone and Olive Ripman, suggested I go to see Braunsweg. When I did so he promptly telephoned Dolin in Paris, saying he thought they should engage me. The previous day Dolin had lunched with Ana Ricarda, the Spanish dancer and choreographer who had danced with me for de Cuevas. For me it was a fortuitous meeting. They had discussed me, and when Dolin expressed his adverse opinion of me, formed at our first meeting, Ana had defended me.

He had obviously thought I was the most ill-mannered little upstart and – being Dolin – had experienced no hesitation in saying so!

Then Ana came to my rescue. 'I think you are making a mistake, Patrick,' she had said. 'I know John, and you have the wrong impression. He is one of the best dancers I've seen. He does a beautiful *Sylphides* and *Nutcracker* pas de deux, which he did in Barcelona with Rosella Hightower.'

I think that more or less decided Dolin upon engaging me. Ana had mentioned the two roles he was rather keen to unload. He was reaching the stage when he no longer wanted to dance the *Nutcracker* Prince, nor *Sylphides*, which he always hated anyway. So in view of what he heard about my dancing he overcame his initial prejudice and decided to give me a chance. I was engaged as principal dancer with the new company, and had the good fortune to be in at the very beginning, with all the excitement of working to help build it.

Not only was Festival Ballet young in its history, but its dancers were also young and dynamic. Youth and freshness were its hallmarks, and there was an abundance of energy and enthusiasm everywhere – on stage, backstage, in the classroom, and from everyone remotely connected with the formation of the new company.

Markova and Dolin at that time formed one of the greatest ever ballet partnerships. They were known throughout the world, so with them at the head of the company our early success was almost assured, and they had gathered about them a group fired with the ambition to bring into being Britain's newest big classical dance company.

Those ten years were extremely hard work, but great fun and a chance to gain the widest possible experience. Dolin and Braunsweg invited all the great ballet stars to the company as guest artists, so that I was able to partner Margot Fonteyn, Tamara Toumanova, Alexandra Danilova, Tatiana Riabouchinska, Carla Fracci, Mia Slavenska, Natalie Krassovska, Yvette Chauvire, Galina Samsova, Toni Lander, Marina Svetlova, and of course Alicia Markova. These in addition to the resident ballerinas such as Belinda Wright and Marilyn Burr. Other partners during my years with Festival Ballet were Irene Shorik, Irina Barowska, Noelle Pontois from the Paris Opera, Nora Kovach (who defected from Hungary with Istvan Rabovsky), and our own Moira Shearer, with whom I danced her last performance when we were in Monte Carlo.

Braunsweg's newly formed company was at first called Gala Performances of Ballet, and for the first two months Markova was unable to dance because of an operation. For me it was a new beginning; the constant challenge and excitement of partnering the succession of guests from whom there was always something to learn, and the stimulation of two seasons a year in London, with the rest of the year on tour.

Soon after I joined the company Dolin decided to whisk me off to Paris to learn *Harlequinade* from Volinine, and for the first time I was exposed to our leading dancer's whirlwind changes of plan and lightning decisions. Anton Dolin rejoices in the given names of Sydney Francis Patrick Chippendall Healey-Kay (Patrick to his friends), and has a volatile Irish temperament. Anyone involved with his travel plans had to have nerves of steel – not least his travel agent. During the last thirty years he has not changed. He is still capable of setting off for New York, being suddenly inspired on the way to the airport, and going to New York via Moscow. Distances and frontiers mean nothing to him. He will arrive from a wearying inter-continental journey, and his only concession to the passing of the years is to collapse into a chair exclaiming, 'I'm exhausted! I really don't know how I do it!' But the wicked twinkle in his eye betrays the fact that he merely needs to stay ten minutes in one place while he plots his next trip. Bright and early next morning he will be badgering telephone operators for instant connection with the four corners of the earth, organising oft-to-be-changed details. On that trip to Paris I thought I was going for two days. How wrong I was! I had not at that time become acquainted with Patrick's unpredictable wanderlust. Once *Harlequinade* was learned, he suddenly had other ideas, and it turned into a whirlwind trip.

We joined his agent, Alfred Katz, for water-skiing at Lugano, then on to Milan, and my first unforgettable sight of Venice, later to become better known and much loved. It was indescribably beautiful in the summer sunshine. Our visit coincided with the annual Carnaval del Luce, when Venice repeats the ceremony of symbolically becoming Bride of the Sea. All the gondolas are hung with lanterns, and huge barges make floating stages for a full orchestra and famous singers. I was twenty, the balcony of my room in the Grand Hotel looked out to the soaring Baroque church of Santa Maria del Salute, poised like a brilliant marble butterfly at the end of the Grand Canal. I was already a well known dancer, the only thing I had ever wanted to be, my career was launched, skimming along under full sail and a favourable wind, and life, during that Venetian summer, seemed pretty marvellous.

I distinctly remember how hot it was. I had my first trip to the Lido, and was whirled off to see Diaghilev's tomb. Venice was full of celebrities. Barbara Hutton had a palazzo opposite the Grand Canal, but decided not to stay in it, choosing instead to stay in our hotel. She was on her honeymoon, having just married Gottfried von Cramm.

One night we had a fairytale trip in a gondola with Jeannette MacDonald, Ella Logan and their husbands. Lanterns hovered over us like fireflies as Patrick said to Jeannette, 'I'm sure everyone is waiting for you to sing.' And sing she did, that lovely, effortless voice floating over the canals, delighting us all on that truly enchanted evening.

Alas, such high moments do not last, and eventually one has to return to earth. After being away for a week, we came back to London to face a barrage of wrath. An irate Leonide Massine had arrived earlier than expected to produce *Le Beau Danube* and was waiting for me to rehearse it with Krassovska. He was furious with Dolin and me because nobody had been told where we were. Because of Massine's early arrival, Julian Braunsweg had been embarrassed at not being able to produce or even contact his principal dancer, so he too was angry, but eventually everyone was placated.

In 1950 we toured Britain, a forerunner of a huge travel programme. Rehearsals started in earnest. Dolin taught me the pas de deux and solo of his *Italian Suite*, the first time he had taught his own role to anyone. The ten-week tour preceding our London debut began in August at the King's Theatre, Southsea, by coincidence the town of my birth. At Markova's suggestion it was decided to call the company Festival Ballet because it was started when the Festival of Britain was being given publicity for the following year. So on 9th October 1950, Festival Ballet, under its new name, made its appearance at the Empire Theatre, Edinburgh, with Markova back after her illness and everybody happy at her return.

Finally, on 24th October, the London season opened at the Stoll Theatre. The company was an instant success, acclaimed by the critics, and played to packed houses. Markova and Dolin danced *Nutcracker*, and Krassovska and I performed *Le Beau Danube*. During that first season Dolin and Nicholas Beriosoff staged a full-length *Nutcracker* and Dolin put on *Giselle*. Markova did not wish to dance more than four or five performances a week, so there began the idea of engaging a succession of guest ballerinas. I was always willing and eager to learn from them as I strove for perfection, with no frills, no showmanship. I had – and still have – a simple love of beauty and of line. A dancer's life may be hard and disciplined, but if that was what was needed, that was what I was prepared for. Our first London season ran until 20th January 1951, and later in the season *Spectre de la Rose* and *Prince Igor* were added to the repertoire.

Once again I found myself dancing that strange, haunting, but so rewarding role in *Spectre*, and again the critics reverted to the Nijinsky comparison they can never resist. This time critics stated what other critics had said, with the result that one paper commented blandly: 'John Gilpin's sensational performance in *Spectre de la Rose* has led critics to compare him with Nijinsky.' Stand up the critic who really saw Nijinsky!

One of the most touching recollections I have of Yvette Chauviré, the great French ballerina, is of a spontaneous and charming gesture she made on the opening night of our first Paris season. She had already danced with the company, and that night was a member of the crowded audience, sitting in a box with Cocteau, Jean Marais and other celebrities.

Spectre went particularly well that night, and the applause was loud and long. Suddenly Chauviré stood up in her box, looked at the audience, indicated the stage and called out, *'Voilà! C'est ça le* vrai *Spectre de la Rose*!'

That is something I shall never forget. A wonderful tribute from a great dancer.

Over the years the role became very closely associated with me. It has now been captured for posterity by sculptor Tom Merrifield's beautiful bronze statuette of me as the Spectre, which stands in the Royal Festival Hall.

Chapter Five

After a short English tour we were all set for our first visit overseas, and went to Monte Carlo in April 1951. It was the first time an English ballet company had appeared there, so to emphasise that fact it was decided to bill the company as London's Festival Ballet. We performed at the beautiful little Opera House holding 600 people, which was built by Garnier, the man responsible for the Paris Opera House. The Monte Carlo Opera House has a great tradition of opera and ballet, and it was there that Diaghilev's Russian Ballet appeared. For Anton Dolin it was a trip down memory lane because in that theatre on New Year's Day, 1924, that he first appeared as Daphnis in *Daphnis and Chloe*. In that same theatre in 1951 David Lichine created *Symphonic Impressions* to a Bizet symphony.

I too had danced in Monte Carlo before, with the de Cuevas company on the occasion of Prince Rainier's coronation. I have particularly nostalgic recollections of that period because of a hilarious drive from Paris to Monte Carlo. My brother was spending a holiday with me, and we joined John Taras in his newly acquired MG sports car for the trip to Monte Carlo. It was a beautiful drive, although not without incident, and it lasted five days, during which we almost wrecked our livers. John Taras is a great gourmet and cannot resist good food, with the result that we stopped at every restaurant of gastronomic note which happened to be en route, sleeping at coaching houses. It was early spring, and the scenery was lovely, culminating in the Côte d'Azure and our first glimpse of the Mediterranean. Somewhere near Fontainebleau John was so busy admiring the scenery that he headed straight for a tree without even noticing.

I saw what was about to happen and frantically grabbed the wheel with the result that we missed the tree but landed in a ditch. Both Tony and I were ill for a week after that unforgettable journey.

After our performance there was a state reception in the ballroom of the royal palace, at which I was presented to the members of Prince Rainier's family, including his sister, Princess Antoinette.

'I know you are English,' she said to me as I was presented, 'and I think you are a beautiful dancer.'

Her compliment brought a blush as she went on to say, 'I would like you to escort me in to dinner.'

It was, of course, a great honour to do so, and as a result of that meeting began a great and enduring friendship. Princess Antoinette and her two daughters, Elizabeth Ann and Christiane Alix, known respectively as Bitsy and Baby, came to rehearsals, starting a habit which carried on throughout all our subsequent visits to Monte Carlo. It soon became obvious that the small Elizabeth Ann only wanted to watch *Spectre de la Rose* – and me. One night when we were in Monte Carlo, Dolin and I went to dine with the Princess at her home in Eze. Bitsy and her small brother Christian Louis (known as Buddy), gave us a private performance in the nursery, doing their best to imitate the dancing they had seen at a matinée a few days previously. At that time Betsy was a delightfully plump, dark-eyed little girl. Later she and her equally enchanting small sister were to have lessons at Susan Debreuil's Monte Carlo ballet school. Susan is an Englishwoman whose husband Jacques played lead viola in the Monte Carlo Orchestra. Years later her son Alain joined Festival Ballet and became a principal dancer.

That 1951 Monte Carlo season was the company's first taste of being fêted. With the brilliant sunshine and spectacular scenery, simply being there was like a holiday, even though we worked hard. Everyone wanted to entertain us, and the audiences at our performances were far more glamorous than anything we offered on stage. They came formally dressed, jewels blazing, tiaras twinkling like stars, and spotting celebrities could have been an endless sport if we had had the time. It seemed the entire jet set of Europe turned out to see us. Playboys, starlets, millionaires and diplomats all thronged to the performances. Only Prince Aly Khan, who frequently arrived with Rita Hayworth, chose comfort rather than formal dress. He turned up in an open-necked shirt!

Our stay ended with a Gala d'Adieu attended by members of the Monaco ruling family, after which we returned for a nine-week season at the Stoll Theatre, where we were in for a period of tantrums and clashing temperaments with all our ballerinas. It was hard to keep the peace and give everyone a fair share of the action. A brave effort was made to distribute roles without bias, but inevitably noses were put out of joint. Krassovska wept when she was told her role of the Street Dancer in *Le Beau Danube* was to be danced by Danilova, who had made it her own. It was originally created by Lydia Lopokova in 1924 in a series of ballet performances in Paris with Massine – *Soirées de Beaumont*, but Danilova made it famous. Shura, as we called Danilova, is one of the few living dancers from the Imperial Russian Ballet of the Maryinsky Theatre of St Petersburg. On stage in 1951 she still had the magical quality of looking like a young girl. Like Markova, she was still dancing brilliantly until well into her forties, the years seeming to leave such stars untouched. I was just twenty-one, and to me Alexandra Danilova was a legend.

When I attended a party to be introduced to her as a new partner I was very much in awe of her, not to say extremely nervous.

At that first meeting she swept her languid eyes over me and exclaimed in her heavy Russian accent, 'My God, he is so young! He had best wear a moustache, otherwise I shall look like his grandmother!'

Needless to say, when we danced together, with Shura's million-dollar legs and bubbling personality, she looked nothing like my grandmother. I was very proud to partner Danilova, who, to my great pleasure, was equally happy to dance with me.

During our three-month season at the Stoll Theatre in 1951, Tatiana Riabouchinska joined the company and Danilova remained as guest ballerina throughout the summer. Dolin put on the famous *Pas de Quatre* with the glittering foursome of Markova, Danilova, Riabouchinska and Krassovska dancing the roles originally created by Marie Taglioni, Carlotta Grisi, Fanny Cerrito and Lucile Grahn. It was a magnificent re-creation of this romantic ballet, and a triumph that the company had four famed ballerinas to perform it so beautifully.

On 31st October 1951 we gave our first Charity Performance, attended by the late Queen Mary, then aged eighty-three. The performance was to honour Dame Adeline Genée and in aid of the Royal Academy of Dancing's Re-building Fund. Our programme consisted of *Capriccioso*, which I danced with Anna Cheselka, *Petrouchka*, and *Les Sylphides* which I danced with Alicia Markova. After the show we were presented to Queen Mary, who had apparently enjoyed it very much.

'Did you know I had lessons from Taglioni?' she said to Alicia afterwards. 'She taught me the Mazurka.'

The Princess Marie Louise graciously agreed to become Patron of the company. She was President of the Three Arts Club, a centre for women in the artistic professions which was at the time in need of funds, so 'her ballet company' as she called us, was asked to give a charity gala at the end of November to help raise money. It was attended by Her Majesty Queen Elizabeth (now the Queen Mother), Princess Margaret, and of course Princess Marie Louise. About a week before the performance Julian Braunsweg gave a star-studded party backstage to publicise the event. The party took place amid the scenery for *Petrouchka*. There were three bars named 'Giselle,' 'Fiesta' and 'Petrouchka', and Jack Buchanan delivered a splendid fund-raising speech to the assembled guests from the top of Petrouchka's booth.

Massine had been invited to dance Petrouchka, but wanted too high a fee for the limited resources of Festival Ballet at that time. Nevertheless, the performance was a glittering affair. The guest artists were Yvette Chauviré and Tania Grantzeva, who replaced Krassovska, given leave of absence to dance in America. We opened with Markova and Dolin in *Les Sylphides*, then I danced *Spectre* with Anita Landa and *Le Beau Danube* with Grantzeva. We had been told that after the performance Queen Elizabeth intended to come on stage in order that the dancers might be presented to her, which was a great thrill. Markova, Dolin, our two guest artists and myself had all been invited to a party to be held later at Lady Annally's flat. The Queen and Princess Margaret would be attending, but we were all sworn to secrecy about the arrangements. Lady Annally was a great balletomane, and never missed our London seasons. She made sure all her friends came too.

When the big moment arrived to be presented, we lined up, fascinated to be able to see the group of 'Royals' at close quarters.

In glamour they far outshone the artists on stage. Queen Elizabeth was in flowing white brocade, ablaze with diamonds, and wearing an ermine cape, looking every inch a queen as she always does. Princess Marie Louise was regal in fox and pearls, and Princess Margaret was a lovely fairy-tale princess.

The supper party afterwards turned out to be a happy, informal affair, with the Queen quickly and charmingly putting us all at our ease. Beatrice Lillie came later from her cabaret appearance at the Café de Paris, arriving with Clifton Webb. When the Queen said how much she would like to hear her sing, Bea demurred, protesting that she did not have her accompanist. By then it was midnight, but Her Majesty was obviously disappointed, so Bea asked Dolin to phone her accompanist, Norman Hackforth, to come immediately – without saying why. That deep resonant voice, later to be so well known as the Mystery Voice on the BBC's *Twenty Questions* could be heard on the other end of the telephone as clearly as if it were in the next room, and Her Majesty was very amused at his evident lack of enthusiasm and determination to go to bed, but Dolin cryptically insisted, so eventually Norman arrived, acutely embarrassed by his refusal to attend when he realised why he had been asked. The evening ended delightfully, with most of us sitting on the floor while Bea sang song after song to the royal requests.

The ballet world is a relatively small one, and old friends keep re-appearing as companies form and re-form. Belinda Wright had been my first partner with Rambert in Australia, and we had first danced together in 1945. We were in Paris together with Roland Petit's company, then after I left she went to America with them. As she wasn't happy there, she wrote to me saying she would like to come to Festival Ballet, so I suggested to Julian Braunsweg that she should be engaged. Julian agreed, and I was delighted to have her back. She joined us in 1951 with Oleg Briansky, also from Petit, and made her first appearance with Festival Ballet at Golders Green Hippodrome.

Belinda is the perfect partner. We always danced marvellously together, with that mysterious alchemy which can sometimes make two dancers a single magnetic force. It was a partnership which always worked beautifully. Now, more than thirty years later, she is still as strikingly attractive, and in addition to her dancing gift has become a talented painter. One of my most prized paintings is one of hers – a delicate Impressionist style study of young lovers.

Vassilie Trunoff and his wife Joan, originally with the Australian

Borovansky company, had danced with Ballet Rambert when we were in Australia. They also wrote to me, and as a result they also came to England to join Festival Ballet. Vassilie is an extremely fine character dancer and he later became ballet master with the company.

The first London season passed in a flash – an undoubted success. Sometimes it was a little difficult to keep the peace as the fiery temperaments of Markova and Dolin often produced sparks, and I was often in the middle of the conflagration. But on the whole the company settled down well together and became a well-knit team, dancers, musicians and stage staff all united in giving of their best. My twin brother Tony joined the company as Assistant Stage Manager in 1951. An accomplished pianist, he could read a musical score, and took to the theatre like a duck to water. He loved the work and rapidly became a very proficient stage manager.

I had a hectic Christmas season, for a time dancing the *Nutcracker* prince at night, and playing matinées in *Where The Rainbow Ends*, with Dolin as St George and myself as that cross between man and dragon, The Slacker.

The world of ballet has its share of dotty characters and glorious eccentrics, as does any other branch of the arts, and one of these was Natalie Krassovska, whom we all loved dearly.

She was of Scottish-Russian descent, and was known as Natalie Leslie before she took on her mother's name of Krassovska. Natalie, or Tata as we called her, was a third generation ballerina. Her grandmother had been a soloist at the Maryinsky Theatre in St Petersburg, and her mother, Lydia Krassovska, was in Diaghilev's company. Tata was born in Russia, had been with the Ballet Russe, and came to Festival Ballet shortly after its inception. One of her great roles, which I danced with her many times, was Giselle. She was a truly beautiful Giselle, but would take about two days to get into the right spiritual mood for her performance. It was never possible to get in touch with her during the forty-eight hours before a *Giselle* performance, and wherever we were on tour she used to spend the entire day in church.

Tata had the habit of saying the most ridiculous things without realising how funny they were, and she caused endless affectionate amusement by the complications in which she involved herself. Her Russian accent grew heavier with the passage of time, and it took her twenty years to become an American citizen simply because she couldn't learn to speak the Declaration which would gain her citizenship.

In New York she had a wedding ceremony at the Russian Orthodox Church, at which she married a musician. After the ceremony came the reception, and all seemed to be perfectly normal and happy. Rumour had it that her new husband disappeared almost immediately, but whatever the situation was, it must have been one of the shortest marriages on record. Perhaps he couldn't stand garlic, which she adored. I discovered this to my cost when I had to dance close to her and received the full blast, and during performances of the Black Swan pas de deux I always suffered terribly!

There was no end to her adventures. On one occasion at the Theatre Royal, Newcastle, she sat on her wash-basin whereupon the basin cracked and flooded the dressing room.

Tata's passport was something else which always caused problems, and she could never find her visa at the right time because she carried it in a tattered plastic bag which had to be unrolled, almost like unrolling a toilet roll. The entire company was invariably held up for at least an hour at Customs because they couldn't discover whether or not she had a visa to enter the country. She once arrived at London Airport from America to do Giselle for us at Festival Hall, and we had a frantic phone call from the airport to say that they had a very strange Russian lady with no work permit who was insisting that she must get to Festival Hall for a rehearsal. Stage Director Benn Toff and I went out to the airport to try and sort things out, and there in the VIP lounge sat Tata, holding court and entertaining everybody. She was wearing a lime green dress over which was a hideous transparent plastic raincoat, and she was covered with fake jewellery, which she adored buying from Woolworth's. The ensemble was completed by two inevitable plastic bags, one of which was full of onions and vegetables.

With total disregard for discretion, considering the fact that she had no visa, she was complaining loudly about the filthy airport food – the steak was overdone and they had no idea how to make a salad. Eventually the Customs department simply capitulated and let her in.

She could be notoriously uncaring about her appearance, but was extremely good-natured about the teasing she received. She simply laughed, or smiled her beautiful smile, and the occasional harsh remarks were like water off a duck's back. Looking into her make-up box was like peering into the depths of an old junk box. It had belonged to her mother, and judging from the age and condition of the make-up it must have dated from Mamma's days in Tsarist Russia! Two days after dancing a classical role, for which she had stuck her hair down at the sides in classical ballerina style, she would have bits of plastic glue adhering to her temples, and the vestiges of her stage make-up of dubious origin. At one point she began to suffer from a rash on her neck, and seemed at a loss to understand why.

When we were in Barcelona Dolin became so furious with her about the condition of her old make-up that one day, without her knowing, he stormed into her dressing room, grabbed the offending make-up box with its mouldering contents, and threw the whole lot into the street. She was naturally very upset when she found out, but at least it had the desired effect of forcing her to go out and buy a complete new set of make-up.

Intentionally or not, she was able to get her own back on Dolin during a performance of *Giselle* in which he was partnering her.

It was at the time when he thought his hair was getting a little thin, so he had a small front hairpiece made up which he combed back into his own hair. He was wearing this small piece of deception during a performance of *Giselle*, at which all was going quite beautifully. Then came the end of the Act II variation where he had to do a double tour, jump, and fall flat on the floor. As he did so the hairpiece flopped over his forehead. Krassovska made her entrance as Giselle in which she had to go over to him and beckon him with an arm gesture. She did it magnificently, but as she did so she flipped the hairpiece, which performed a lovely small arc in the air, much to the amusement of the audience. Act II of *Giselle* is anything but humorous, and this broke the spell completely. The hairpiece was left on stage, and Dolin was enraged at the whole incident.

When we were in the States on one of our tours, Tata wished to make a trip to Montreal. She sought advice about the best plane to catch as she wished to drop off at Miami, Florida, on the way.

'But you can't do that!' she was told. 'It's a completely different direction.'

(*Above*) Tamara Toumanova, one of Festival Ballet's guest ballerinas, as Odette in *Swan Lake*, 1952.

(*Right*) With Alexandra Danilova in Festival Ballet's production of *Le Beau Danube,* 1951—an autographed photograph.

(*Left*) With Alicia Markova
the *Blue Bird pas de deux*
the Stoll Theatre, 1952.

(*Below*) *Giselle* with Alici
Markova at the Stoll Thea
1952.

'I've done it,' replied Tata. 'It can be done.'

'Nonsense.'

Tata was insistent that she had already made a similar trip on a previous occasion, but then it was pointed out to her that the previous year she had flown from New York to Lima, Peru, and stopped off at Miami. That made sense; was she not thinking of that?

Her face broke into a beautiful smile, all argument forgotten.

'That's it,' she said triumphantly. 'Now I remember.'

Travel was not her strong point. She was terribly seasick when crossing the Channel on one occasion, and managed to elicit a lot of sympathy.

'You poor darling,' said one of the group. 'What on earth are you going to do if we go on tour to America?'

Tata raised a sickly green and miserable face, haggard with Russian drama. 'I hope they will take us by train,' she gasped tragically.

Dolin was always intent upon making Tata presentable to his high standards. We were once appearing in Paris during a big international theatre festival, and had been invited to attend a reception given by the Ambassador. We were often invited to very grand occasions and this was one of them. Festival Ballet was chosen to represent British dance, Laurence Olivier and Viven Leigh were there with the Old Vic Company, and it was quite obvious every member of our company was going to dress to kill. Dolin decided that this was one time when Tata was not going to be left to her own devices as far as appearance went. He dragged her off to Balmain for a new gown, deaf to any protests, and blind to the expense.

Dolin was determined that Tata, as our prima ballerina, was going to turn up looking absolutely ravishing, as indeed she could. She had two beautiful dresses made at Balmain, one in the inevitable lime green, which for some reason was one of her favourite colours. The reception was a glittering affair, and among the well-dressed company Tata presented herself in her new creation, looking quite exquisite. She had gone to endless trouble, and her lovely Madonna-like face was superbly made up. Unfortunately she must have pulled her dress on over her already made-up face, and her beautiful Balmain gown was smothered in mascara! But whatever her social gaffes we all loved her, and she must have returned our affections because every time she went away, she made the touching gesture of bringing back a small gift for each member of the company upon her return.

At the time of our second visit to Monte Carlo Dolin had gone to the States, among other things to see about the possibility of taking the company to America. Because of a series of mishaps on the return journey he arrived late in Monte Carlo, totally exhausted, and informed Markova that he would not be partnering her on the opening night of *Nutcracker*. Instead she would be dancing with me.

Perhaps naturally she seemed upset, especially because her foot was troubling her again, but reluctantly agreed to dance. For some unaccountable reason, that performance of *Nutcracker* seemed to me mechanical, and at the climax of the coda in Act II, when she had to jump into my arms, it felt as if she had collapsed over my shoulder. I was extremely angry to read in the papers next day that it looked as if I had dropped her, which wasn't true at all.

I had always been afraid that my relationship with Markova would not be a successful one and now this seemed to me to have happened.

I could not help wondering whether perhaps she had been reluctant to dance with me because of the wide difference in our ages despite her very youthful appearance and being – as she is to this day – a very beautiful woman with a ballerina's classical grace, and that ageless quality which the best of them retain. She remains one of the greatest romantic ballerinas of this century.

Alicia's sister Doris, an ex-Windmill showgirl, was her publicist, ally, and reinforcement in her differences with Dolin, and Doris always backed her to the hilt. The next day Doris announced that Markova was leaving the company. Her foot was bad and she must leave for London. There was nothing that could be done about it, and Alicia went.

The atmosphere became more relaxed, although some of the company thought we would be unable to carry on without Markova, and Fate had not finished with us yet! Three days later Dolin injured his knee while dancing, a calamity which prevented him from performing for three months. His knee was the size of a melon, but he had himself wheeled to rehearsals each day. Lying on the floor, he managed to teach Oleg Briansky his solo and coda from the *Don*

Quixote pas de deux. This was Oleg's first big opportunity and set him on the road to fame as a dancer. Colette Marchand replaced Markova, and somehow between us, Oleg, Colette, Krassovska and I, with Riabouchinska and the company, carried the season to success, with the support of our enthusiastic Monte Carlo audiences.

After the season we had two weeks free. Dolin and I had previously agreed to dance at a charity ball at St Moritz, so Patrick took the opportunity of visiting Swiss doctors for his injured knee, and I had the chance to meet Viennese singer Greta Keller, who taught me to ski.

I took to it like a penguin to a snowdrift and it was not long before I was whizzing happily and heedlessly down the slopes while Patrick stayed fuming on the terrace, nursing his bad leg. He was terrified in case I broke a leg, and every time he saw somebody brought in on a stretcher he was sure it was a battered and incapacitated Gilpin. Happily, I remained in one piece, although I suppose I was both thoughtless and foolhardy to take such risks at that time, when I might so easily have produced the third disaster of the series.

When it came to the charity gala, Patrick, in great pain, somehow managed to dance a couple of improvisations while Greta sang, and very reluctantly I danced two terrifying solos on the highly and dangerously polished ballroom floor. I always hated being asked to dance off-stage, because ballet is totally different from cabaret, and in my opinion never works without the ordered space of a stage.

Our arrival back in London heralded a nomadic existence of constant tours. Patrick began to dance again, and although at first he had to rely upon his magnificent showmanship to help him through the roles, as his strength came back and his knee recovered, he was soon dancing again at the top of his form. We had a month's season at the Stoll Theatre before touring the provinces, but on 30th July 1952 we opened at what was to become our permanent London home, the Royal Festival Hall. Built as a concert hall, it only became possible for ballet because of Benn Toff's brilliant idea of building a vast portable stage on the system of a Bailey Bridge.

Benn was a marvellous stage director, so loyal to the company up to the time he died. He was devoted to Julian Braunsweg, and to the ballet. The Festival Hall stage is difficult to negotiate because there is no wing space, and in ballets like *Giselle* it is a nightmare to get the corps de ballet off, round the back, and on again from a different direction. Dancers become more exhausted rushing round the back at the Royal Festival Hall than as a result of what they do on stage. But the Bailey Bridge stage was a brilliant invention, and Festival Ballet would not be what it is today if it had not been for pioneers like Benn Toff.

Tamara Toumanova, whom I partnered in 1952, was one of the great Russian dancers to appear with the company. With Tatiana Riabouchinska and Irina Baronova she was one of the three 'baby ballerinas' with Colonel de Basil's Ballets Russes de Monte Carlo during the Thirties, and it was into this area of mature professionalism that I was catapulted head first when I was a twenty-one-year-old principal dancer. I could not claim to be a Russian, nor a defector with the glamour of escape from behind the Iron Curtain – I was a home-grown product – an English boy from Devonshire.

When Dolin insisted I again partner Markova in *Nutcracker* I still felt that the partnership would be unhappy. As day after day passed without a rehearsal, I grew increasingly nervous because I wanted it to be perfect. I also knew my position was very vulnerable, and how easily this great opportunity – which it was for me – could be ruined by the slightest mishap. It would no doubt be put down to my youth, my inexperience, my inadequacy in some direction, and the fault would probably be laid at my door. When it came to a clash of wills between Markova and Dolin, lesser mortals were advised to keep out of range. Unfortunately, this time I was in the middle of it. The performance, only days away, was still unrehearsed, and I was practically a nervous wreck. Dolin had to consider announcing Markova's indisposition and replacement by Krassovska, but fortunately Alicia recovered and in the end everything went beautifully, but it was a great relief to go on holiday to Capri – my first visit to that spectacular island, where for the first time I met Gracie Fields at her lovely home, the Canzone del Mare.

Although she liked the quiet life, Gracie's soft heart always made her give in to the pleas of her many fans who found their way to her, and she would respond happily to their request, 'Give us a song!' She never changed, and was as happy to perform 'The Ugly Duckling' to an audience of one small boy as she was to break into 'Sing As We

Go' for the benefit of a group of enraptured tourists. She made the island so much her own that the sight of Gracie leaning nonchalantly against a balustrade, belting out 'Sally' with that rich Lancashire accent, against the exotic background of the Faraglioni and the Mediterranean, was not even incongruous. At the same time I met Gloria, an ebullient character who kept a nearby restaurant which was patronised by all the visiting celebrities. That holiday was enlivened by the presence of Sophie Tucker. Margot Fonteyn was there, Frederick Ashton, and Ruth Page . . . in all it was a magic time.

But halcyon days in the refuge of an enchanted island have to be few, and we were soon back to rehearsals and the beginning of our next tour, which was to herald a series of disasters. Rehearsing in Glasgow with Dolin, Markova hurt her foot. She pluckily carried on, but her ankle swelled to such proportions she had to return to London for treatment. After a brief holiday we were due to appear in Monte Carlo for the second time, and two of our faithful fans, who had been to every performance of our London season, arranged to come with us. Olive and Doreen Mills, two sisters from Leyton, had been at the stage door of the Stoll Theatre each night, and they happened to say to Julian Braunsweg that they wished they could be at the stage door in Monte Carlo. To repay their loyalty he said they could go as part of the company. Olive was a typist, and Doreen was a designer. They saved up their expenses, got a theatrical return ticket for about £20 and the company paid the rest. When we opened in Monte Carlo on Christmas Day, 1951 with *Nutcracker*, our two faithful followers were there to see it.

I had to wear a wig in that production of *Nutcracker*, and I always hated wigs. With the difficulty of anchoring them to my short hair I was always afraid of them slipping to a comical angle. Eventually I dispensed with the wig and evolved an alternative of plastering my hair with white Meltonian shoe cream and lacquer, and then sprinkling it with glitter dust. This was later copied by Irina Kolpakova and the Russians when we shared a Royal Albert Hall season in 1963. Years afterwards, when we did *Witch Boy*, having worn a hated wig once and vowed never to do so again, somebody suggested using a temporary rinse to darken my hair. During the first solo, when I was bathed in perspiration, the rinse started to run and so did my mascara, all the black goo ending up agonisingly in my eyes so that I couldn't see! From then on for performances of *Witch Boy* I took a stick of black greasepaint, smeared it on my hands and rubbed it into my hair so that it was uniformly black. Unlike actors who play the same role night after night, a dancer's change of hair colour has to be temporary, and the most convenient answer has to be found.

Chapter Six

In the beginning, the engagement of a constant flow of guest stars had meant that startlingly original works had to be cut to a minimum. The bedrock of the repertoire was formed by the classics – *Giselle, Nutcracker*, the most important Fokine works, Massine's *Le Beau Danube, Napoli* and Beriosoff's version of *Esmeralda*. Gradually new ballets were introduced, and one of the great successes was *Symphony For Fun*, which had its first performance in September 1952 at the Royal Festival Hall. The choreography was by Michael Charnley, who was trained by Jooss, and the music was 'Symphony No 5½' by Don Gillis. It was a lively, jazzy ballet and very good for the company at that time because it brought out Festival Ballet's youthful exuberance and gave the company a stamp of originality. It was part of our programme when we gave our first performance in Copenhagen some time later, and the Danes loved it, as indeed did most audiences. We often had to give an encore of the last movement.

Marilyn Burr, whom I was later to partner on many occasions, joined the company in Edinburgh as a member of the corps de ballet. Eight weeks later she suddenly shot into the limelight because Natalie Krassovska hurt her foot during a performance. Later in the programme she was billed to dance the Black Swan pas de deux with me, but felt she was unable to do so because of her foot. Dolin approached Marilyn and asked if she knew Black Swan. She replied that she did, and was promptly told that she was to go on in that role in about ten minutes. Naturally she was petrified, but had little time to think about it.

We had a hasty rehearsal in Dolin's dressing room, and Marilyn went forth to dance her first major role with Festival Ballet. She later became a soloist, and then principal dancer, but she seemed prone to receiving last minute demands. She was telephoned one morning when we were at Leicester and told to get to the theatre immediately because Krassovska was ill and she was going to have to dance Giselle that evening. When Marilyn duly arrived at the theatre the stage was being set, and there was no opportunity of a stage rehearsal, so Dolin put her through her paces in the aisle, between the front row and the orchestra pit. After four hours there, we were finally able to have a stage rehearsal and the evening's *Giselle* was a great success, despite Marilyn's intense nervousness.

Paris beckoned in 1953, and we had a four-week season at the Theatre de l'Empire, during which we gave a 'Homage to Fokine' evening with *Sylphides, Spectre de la Rose, Schéhérazade* and *Prince Igor*. On the last night of that season Yvette Chauviré made the charming gesture of sending each girl in the corps de ballet a posy of flowers. It was a wonderful audience, and they stood and clapped and cheered for twenty minutes.

Negotiations had been in progress for a tour of Canada and after our provincial tour in the spring we left for a Coronation season of two weeks in Canada, playing Montreal, Toronto, Quebec and Ottawa. We were in Montreal at the time of the Coronation, and indeed, I always seem to be out of the country for our great national ceremonial occasions. In 1977, at the time of the Silver Jubilee celebrations I was in Pittsburgh as Director of the Pittsburgh Ballet, and I waited up all night in my room at the Ritz Carlton Hotel for the film to be flown in for television showing. There was a great race as to whether Canada or America would receive the film first, and the Canadians won. As I sat and watched the television film I felt very nostalgic and homesick for London, and as I was already very depressed at the time, the film did nothing to help.

While we were in Canada for the Coronation tour we rehearsed *Alice in Wonderland* which Michael Charnley had choreographed to music by Joseph Horovitz. Belinda Wright was Alice, Keith Beckett was The Mad Hatter, and I was The White Rabbit. It was quite a change to be doing a character part instead of the traditional classics, and great fun. A Tiger-Lily/Dragon Fly pas de deux had been arranged for Sonia Arova and Oleg Briansky, but as rehearsals progressed it became quite obvious that the ballet was going to be too long, so Dolin as Director cut out the Arova pas de deux. It was the cue for a storm to break, and it did so. Arova was furious, but Dolin was adamant that the pas de deux must go, so she called a press conference and promptly threatened to sue the company for 25,000 dollars. Needless to say, that kind of money was not available in Festival Ballet at that time – or at any subsequent time, and the storm eventually passed.

Alice had its première at the Pavilion Theatre, Bournemouth on 2nd July 1953. It was a great romp, and one week later we gave the first London performance at the Royal Festival Hall.

I always hated the *Alice* costume, even though the ballet was fun. It had a mask depicting a rabbit's head, and was made of heavy wool. In the summer heat of the Royal Festival Hall it was positively stifling. I am sorry *Alice* did not remain in the repertoire because it would have made a lovely Christmas ballet. Instead, every company pulls out the perennial *Nutcracker*.

The rhythm of overseas tours accelerated. We went to Italy, starting in Naples at the lovely San Carlo Opera House, which was like the inside of a lavishly decorated hat-box, tier rising upon tier. It was my first experience of the Italian genius for organising total chaos and expecting a show to come out of it – as surprisingly, it usually does. We had endless orchestra troubles during the tour, sometimes ending up by dancing to our conductor's singing as the locally recruited musicians petered out, unable to cope with the score.

Our musical director and conductor was Geoffrey Corbett, and we all had to contend with the Italian preference for opera rather than ballet. Puccini operas were so much more acceptable to them than Tchaikovsky ballets, so the musicians were not always familiar with many of the ballet scores. Geoffrey Corbett did a wonderful job with the music, but at the first performance of *Le Beau Danube* the Italian musicians decided they were not going along with Strauss, and many of them simply stopped playing. With lightning presence of mind, Geoffrey rushed to the piano and kept things going by playing the music himself.

At the Teatro La Fenice in Venice, the most beautiful theatre in which I have ever danced, many of the audience arrived by private gondolas. It never occurs to an Italian audience that a performance will begin on time. They usually arrived by the second interval, the women be-furred and be-jewelled, with no intention whatever of taking their seats. Instead, they either stand up to see or be seen, or circulate among their friends, chattering animatedly. A quite magnificent spectacle, and all part of the local colour. Even great fun, in small doses!

One needs a nervous system tempered with the resilience of a steel spring to cope with the vicissitudes likely to arise in an Italian theatre. That tour also included Florence, Turin, Modena, Bologna, Parma, Biella, and the Teatro Olympico in Vincenza. This was built by Palladio and was a spectacular setting for such ballets as *Swan Lake* and *Les Sylphides*.

And so the company danced (and Geoffrey Corbett sang!) its way through Italy. When an orchestra faltered and petered out, the intrepid Geoffrey's voice would rise encouragingly from the orchestra pit. The audience loved it, having a natural affection for singers. They began to clap in time while we went on dancing.

Some years later, in 1964, I was to dance in another Roman arena, that of Verona, in a full-length production of *Swan Lake* with Galina Samsova and Lucette Aldous. I was never bothered by stage fright, but for some reason in that vast arena I was really scared. There was an audience of 30,000, and no curtains of course. Lights were turned on to the audience to dazzle them and conceal the scene changes, and as they were turned on to the stage I was sure I knew exactly how gladiators felt when about to enter the arena. The area was enormous! There were 400 extra dancers and an orchestra of 150, including musicians from La Scala and La Fenice. We had four weeks of rehearsals in blinding heat, and the choreography had to be extended to cover the mammoth arena. The members of the audience were given candles to light in order to read their programmes, and they pin-pointed the perimeter of the dark arena like so many flickering fireflies.

In 1953, during our holiday month of September, Anton Dolin and I were asked to dance in a short tour of India arranged by Marina Svetlova, our guest ballerina at Festival Ballet. Her husband, Theodore Haig, a concert pianist, was to be our accompanist. I did not want to have my anti-cholera injections before the end of the Festival Ballet season in case the reaction would interfere with my dancing, so I had the anti-cholera and anti-typhoid injections immediately after the last performance. The others had their injections at the same time with the result that we all had the reactions on the plane to India. My arm swelled up like a balloon and I developed a raging temperature. I felt so ill that I had to spend two days in bed. Luckily we were having two weeks' holiday in Ceylon first, so a few days of sun-bathing and swimming in the warm waters of the Indian Ocean soon had me back in form.

We arrived in Colombo, and our opening was to be in Bombay. During our illness brought on by our inoculations we had overlooked one vital factor – we had not rehearsed! So on the beach, when the tide had gone out leaving the sand damp and firm, we would jump up from our sun-bathing and rehearse. At night we did further rehearsals on the hotel ballroom floor.

Marina Svetlova, who had done many tours with a small group of dancers known as the Marina Svetlova Ensemble, had been used to arranging her own lighting effects for the group. She accordingly took care of our lighting in the absence of a stage manager.

In Bombay, when she wanted to arrange a rehearsal, she found a small group of Hindus sitting at the theatre surrounded by a selection of old lighting gelatines, all ready to start. They seemed to be almost affronted at the idea of a lighting rehearsal.

'No, no, we do not need rehearsal,' they insisted.

'But how can you not need a rehearsal,' argued Marina. 'You don't even know what we are doing.'

'Oh, we had a ballerina here before, we know what to do,' they protested.

'When was that?' asked Marina.

'In 1920.'

Marina could not believe her ears.

'Who was it?' she asked, amazed.

'Anna Pavolva,' came the reply.

They continued to squat exactly where they were, and eventually Marina persuaded them to give us a lighting rehearsal, using the same equipment which had been used for Pavlova more than thirty years previously.

Just before the first performance, while we were putting on our make-up, a young fourteen-year-old boy showed up. He was very anxious to see the performance, but could not afford a ticket, so he sent a message to Dolin asking if he might be permitted to watch from the side of the stage.

We talked to him afterwards. He was absolutely fascinated by the performance, and came to each one. 'I am not staying in this country,' he stated firmly. 'One day I am going to America.' He was nothing if not ambitious, and time brought his ambitions to fruition, because that young boy was Zubin Mehta, who became conductor of the Israel Philharmonic Orchestra, and a musician known throughout the world.

In two weeks in India we gave thirteen performances, which was a taxing schedule as there was no corps de ballet and everything fell upon our shoulders. There was also a constant run of parties, and it seemed that performances were squeezed in between socialising. We became acutely aware of the difference between rich and poor in India. At the parties we would meet well dressed, rich men and beautiful women, ablaze with jewellery, and afterwards we would be told cars were waiting to take us back to our hotel. We felt in desperate need of fresh air, and always offered to walk back, but our hosts would never hear of it. We realised they did not want us to walk because we would see the poverty – which indeed we did, and it was appalling. When we were allowed to walk through the streets we found ourselves having to step over the hungry, the beggars, and the lepers sitting in the roadways.

In New Delhi we danced before Prime Minister Nehru and his sister Mrs Pandit, who came to several of our performances.

We had a day off to visit the Taj Mahal, but were almost too tired to enjoy it. Finally we were dropped at the side of a swimming pool, where we simply collapsed and lazed in the sun. After flying back to England we landed in London and then made our way to Oxford by train, where Marina Svetlova and I danced the first ballet of the evening programme. India seemed a million miles away, yet twenty-four hours previously we had been in that very different world.

The incessant travelling with Festival Ballet produced many bizarre and amusing incidents. Flying over the moutains during one of our South American trips we hit a patch of turbulence above some of the highest peaks, and the plane began to bob up and down like a yo-yo for about thirty minutes as the heat of the Argentinian Plain met the intense cold of the Andes. There were some members of the company who could never accustom themselves to rough travel conditions, and were apt to panic when aeroplanes behaved in temperamental fashion when in the air, or showed some reluctance to leave the ground. We encountered both contingencies on our tours from time to time. I happened to be in the lavatory when the plane suddenly dropped about 2,000 feet. I shot up in the air as if yanked by an invisible wire, hit my head on the ceiling, and was deposited again with great precision on to the loo seat from which I had been so unceremoniously lifted. Being blessed with a total immunity to travel sickness, I emerged from the small room wreathed in smiles at the thought of the ludicrous picture I must have made, only to be greeted by expressions of pronounced hostility by the rest of the company, who were sporting various degrees of pallor, from travel sickness or fright, and irritated by my insouciance.

With all the travelling we did, I suppose toilet facilities played quite a major part in our lives, and we had a hilarious 38-hour journey from Warsaw to East and West Berlin, and no lavatory on the train! We arrived at East Berlin in the morning, and were just allowed out on to the platform. Back on the train, we were immediately closed in and all doors were locked.

Despite being as stiff as rusty roller-skates after such a long period sitting still, we had to dance that night. Next day as we boarded the bus at Hildersheim we expressed the hope that there would not be a repetition of the previous day's discomfort.

'Oh don't worry,' the Company's General Manager said airily, 'Stuttgart isn't very far.'

With that assurance ringing in our ears we piled into the bus, fortified by liquid refreshment. John Auld, later ballet master with Festival Ballet, was a most congenial travelling companion on that trip, and we all arrived at Stuttgart in various advanced stages of inebriation. When the bus doors were finally opened, dozens of beer cans rolled out and went clattering down the road, much to the stupefaction of the local inhabitants!

Looking back over that rich tapestry of travels, we were like a troupe of modern day troubadours, working our way round the British Isles, Europe, USA, South America, the Middle East, and even further afield. We danced in famous opera houses, provincial theatres, historic arenas, and on rough, improvised stages. Our audiences too were just as varied as the theatres themselves. We played to sophisticated houses, heads of state, members of the jet set who cared nothing for ballet, but came to be seen, balletomanes who saved for months to pay for their seats, and those having their first experience of ballet. And we loved it all.

Our tours of Portugal always seemed to coincide with elections or political crises, with their attendant riots and curfews. We therefore often found ourselves running the gauntlet from the theatre to our hotel with armed troops grimly manning barricades. May Day was always particularly hazardous with its parades and scuffles. During one of our May seasons we encountered soldiers on horseback, rushing up and down the streets with sabres. We were always warned not to go out, but some of the company took the risk and came back with their clothes ruined – spattered with blue dye thrown during a street riot. It took days to get it off skin and clothes.

Lisbon, where we made annual appearances at the beautiful San Carlo Opera House, seemed to be the setting for some of our spectacular exploits. We had been to a Portuguese Fado party one night,and were pleasantly 'high' on Portuguese vino. Our hotel was in the square, on a hill, and in the middle of the square work was in progress. Paving stones were being laid, and there were several cement mixers standing around. These were not like English cement mixers, but were open troughs, below the level of the pavement on which we were walking.

We were all in great humour. I felt beautifully heady, and was dancing happily along the street with the others. I suppose I was showing off, prancing and balancing, when I missed my footing, slipped, and went straight down into one of the cement mixers – which was full! There was a mixture of consternation and hysterical inebriated laughter among my companions as they hauled me out. It was quite a hot evening, and they thought it advisable to get me back to the hotel before my cement coating began to set. The idea of being stoned suddenly took on a whole new meaning as I soaked off the gritty residue in a hot bath.

There always seemed to be marvellous parties. One year we had finished the season on the continent and started our holidays. Lucette Aldous, her husband and myself went to a Portuguese nightclub where we stayed until about five in the morning. We were leaving for London that day, but at 5 a.m. decided to go to the beach at Estoril. Two others joined us, and I have no recollection of how we got to Estoril, but somehow we arrived at the beach, feeling delightfully merry. Exhausted, we fell asleep on the sand as dawn came up. Not only did dawn come up, but the sun rose too while we continued to sleep. At two in the afternoon I woke up, burned to a cinder, as was everyone else. Not only were we badly scorched through sleeping for hours under a blazing sun, but we had missed the plane back to England. There was only one thing to do, and we did it – we decided to stay on another week!

I have always been a sun-worshipper, and it has never been difficult for me to collect a sun tan, but that experience remains in my memory as the most painful burning I have ever received from a merciless sun.

I have talked elsewhere in this book about Ballet Mothers, and on our 1954 North America tour we had two Ballet Mothers par excellence. Two of our guest ballerinas on that tour were Tamara Toumanova and Violette Verdy, and both were chaperoned by their mothers, who naturally did not take to each other because each believed that her daughter was the greatest ballerina ever to put on a pair of pointe shoes.

Toumanova's mother, Eugenie, was the daughter of a noble Russian family who had fled the Revolution and Tamara was born in a troop truck on the way to Vladivostok – it is one of those improbable stories which has the merit of truth. Toumanova Senior was deeply into Spiritualism, fortune-telling, and table-rapping communications with the spirit of Nijinsky. On the other hand she was an inveterate gambler, and as our private train rumbled across the territories of North America she was to be found incarcerated in a compartment with the musicians, losing a fortune at poker. She would appear at approximately hourly intervals to have her dwindling assets replenished by her daughter, and by the time we reached California she had lost about 3,000 dollars.

The feud between our two ballet mothers continued for much of the tour, and the only time they were in any way united was when the company had bad notices in Chicago, and they were so busy defending their respective daughters they overlooked the fact that for once they were in agreement about something. Eventually one of them left and the tour continued more peacefully.

It was a tremendous tour, through Canada, and then a coast to coast tour of the United States, where we did twenty-eight one-night stands, sometimes two performances a day.

We had our own train, which was like a travelling hotel. There was a 'club car' with a bar, four sleeping carriages and four 90-feet railway wagons for the scenery. Fending off boredom became a problem, during all the travelling. Apart from the resident gamblers there were those who played Monopoly, those who talked, and those who slept. The evenings when we were travelling and not performing we had gatherings during which we managed a party atmosphere, and played records on Benn Toff's new portable record player. The continual moving gave many headaches to the stage crew. Every theatre was different, and the schedules were often so tight that it seemed impossible that the sets would be unloaded, erected, struck again after the performance and re-loaded in time for the next one, but somehow they always were. We arrived in Richmond, Virginia, in the middle of a blizzard, and with snow six feet deep. The theatre for the night was a school gymnasium and the fire brigade had to be called in to hose the snow away from the entrance and clear a path for us to get in.

Greensboro, North Carolina, was a one night stand, and after the performance we all descended upon the only café we could find. The owner, although delighted at the sudden influx of trade, was unable to cope with the hungry hordes, but Toumanova and her mother both rose to the occasion. They gamely took over behind the counter and began to cook hamburgers as thought they had done it all their lives. From there we went by hired bus to Raleigh, two hours away, but it began to snow again and we could not see through the bus windows. We crawled along, reaching our destination at six o'clock in the morning, utterly exhausted, piling out of the bus into more snow, about two feet deep.

We all slept until lunchtime and then went to the theatre to rehearse. All the shops in the town had closed, and the local population had taken to impromptu winter sports because that was the first snow they had ever seen.

It was almost Christmas when we were in San Francisco. We did *Petrouchka* with Dolin in the title role and Stravinsky conducting his own score. It was a great event to have the composer in the orchestra pit, but he conducted as though he were in a concert hall and the

ectre de la Rose with Moira
earer, Monte Carlo,
uary, 1954.

s Sylphides with Margot
onteyn, Monte Carlo,
nuary, 1956

(*Left*) Festival Ballet, 1959. *Les Sylphides* with Carla Fracci.

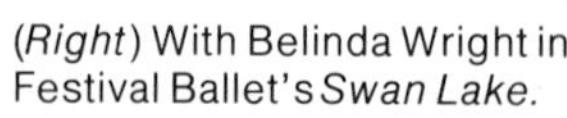

(*Right*) With Belinda Wright in Festival Ballet's *Swan Lake.*

tempos were not ideal for the ballet, which produced a few problems. There were lots of Press photographers around, all dying to get a shot of Stravinsky, but he absolutely refused to have any photographs taken of himself.

Christmas saw us in Los Angeles, and we met all the famous movie stars who turned out for our performance. We spent a short holiday in California, and the whole company stayed at the Ambassadors Hotel in Hollywood. I moved out for a time and stayed with my brother with Ella Logan and her husband. The tour then started again shortly after Christmas at San Diego. Long hours of travelling, travel-stiffness, and having to perform one-night stands with no real chance to loosen up are terrible problems for dancers.

In Cleveland, Ohio we had the novel experience of dancing in a theatre which was really two entertainment centres under one roof, divided by an iron curtain. On the other side of the division a circus was performing, and every evening during our last ballet a woman was shot from a cannon into the circus ring with a deafening explosion. We began to wait for it, and it was impossible to keep a straight face when the inevitable shot was fired.

Although the Chicago critics were not the kindest at least they had a sense of humour. The ballet they favoured most was *Schéhérazade*, which they loved. One critic described it as 'the sexiest show in years', adding that had it not been 'art' the cops would have instantly closed it. The notice added, 'There will be another performance on Saturday. Opera glasses will be on hire from the desk. Goody!'

In 1955 Festival Ballet produced *Etudes*, a ballet by Harald Lander, who had originally mounted it for the Royal Danish Ballet in 1948. The music was by Czerny, and it was a 'fireworks' ballet which became one of the mainstays of Festival's repertoire, and one of the ballets for which I was best known.

One of the questions I have often been asked during the course of my career is whether I have been influenced by any particular dancer. The answer is that no one person has ever influenced me. I have taken a great deal from various dancers, but not with the idea of copying them. At the back of my mind I have always had my own ideas about how things should be done, although I have gleaned much from great teachers like Volkova. My ideal is that dancing should be kept 'pure and simple'; when a part calls for flamboyance then one brings it out, but only when the music demands, and even then there are ways and means of doing it.

Etudes is a great virtuoso ballet, and when I was rehearsing it I felt the music demanded that the big pirouette section should be danced non-stop. Up to then, other dancers had stopped after each series of pirouettes, and I felt it killed the whole continuity. I worked and worked on it until I was able to do it on stage non-stop. There are then thirty-two fouettés, which are very rare for a man to do anyway, so it was quite a tour de force. Nobody has done it since, but I had to do it because it was logical and in the music. That was the sole motivation.

Throughout my life my performances have always been motivated by music, which I love to listen to even when not directly related to the ballet. During my career there have been some truly great moments of music, heightened by the occasion on which they were heard. One was at the International Eisteddfod in Llangollen where we danced in 1953. I shall never forget the representatives from all countries on stage singing 'Land of my Fathers' in that stupendous setting of towering green moutains, waterfalls, rushing rivers and verdant valleys. Then there were the exquisite open air settings afforded by an Israeli night, proof that Tchaikovsky is perhaps the most perfect of ballet composers.

There is nothing so lush and beautiful as his music for the *Nutcracker* pas de deux. The 'Aurora' pas de deux from *The Sleeping Beauty* needs the whole ballet behind it in order to climb to the big pas de deux of the wedding scene, but that from *Nutcracker* can stand alone. It is really for the Sugar Plum Fairy, and has to be grand, yet at the same time have a kind of fragility about it. I cannot count the number of times I have danced *Nutcracker*, and it has had so many versions. Now, unfortunately, I see numerous performances which seem to bear no relation at all to the real *Nutcracker*, especially the pas de deux. Unlike the one in the second act of *Swan Lake* it is not a love duet, and should never be danced as such. All it needs is a clear interpretation.

Alicia Markova was the most wonderful Sugar Plum Fairy. Her realisation of it was exactly right; it must be like crystal. With Markova it always was.

I have had some wonderful partners during my long association with *Nutcracker*, each bringing something different to the role of the Sugar Plum Fairy. Belinda Wright, with whom I danced it countless times with Festival Ballet, was always beautiful. It is not an easy role in that it has to have a certain gentleness as well as the grandeur which goes with the music.

The 'Black Swan' variation is another piece in which the music demands a somewhat flashy interpretation, but it should also have great elegance. I well recall a gala in 1954 when Kovach and Rabovsky were guest artists with Festival Ballet and were dancing at the performance to celebrate our fifth anniversary. Istvan Rabovsky was noted for his strong Russian technique, and was a great sensation for his ability to do sixteen double tours in a row. At the gala he and Nora Kovach danced the *Don Quixote* pas de deux, full of lifts, spins and leaps. They were a huge success, especially when he came on and promptly performed his sixteen double tours, which the audience had been waiting for. They went wild with appreciation, and I remember thinking as I watched, 'To me this is acrobatics and not dancing.'

The roars and shouts of applause finally died away, and Krassovska and I were on immediately afterwards with 'Black Swan', which is far more flamboyant in the concert version than in the actual ballet because the mime with Rothbart does not detract from the dancing itself.

I went on stage completely in control of myself, determined to keep it elegant, but then the excitement began to build. The audience had been warmed up by Rabovsky, and were now looking for fireworks, prepared to applaud everything. When it came down to the Coda, Krassovska and I simply hurled ourselves into it, doubling everything, and bringing the house down for the second time that evening.

Krassovska left the company in 1955, and one of our guest ballerinas was Ludmilla Tcherina who, with Edmond Audran, danced at our gala a ballet choreographed by Audran to Sibelius's *Swan of Tuonela*. Unfortunately Tcherina hurt her foot during a rehearsal, and it was touch and go whether she would be able to dance. Tcherina had her own remedy for such disasters, and must have used it many times before because she was totally confident.

She acquired a piece of raw meat, which she stuffed in her point shoe, and danced the performance perfectly.

Tcherina brought with her a great film star glamour, but despite her reputation on celluloid I never thought of her as a great ballerina. She always looked magnificent, and I would often see her at the beach in Monte Carlo wearing her turbans and exquisite beach clothes. She did a terrifying solo to Rimsky-Korsakov's 'Flight of the Bumble Bee', and had mirrors at the side of the stage so that she could see what she was doing. She even brought glamour into the classroom, sometimes wearing vivid pink leotards. She arrived one day at a class in Paris looking fabulous, her wrists covered in gold bracelets.

We did the barre exercises and started centre practice when, halfway through the adage she stopped the class and said apologetically in French, 'I must take off these bracelets. They are much too heavy.' At which she proceeded to strip off the bracelets and place them on the piano in leisurely fashion while we all watched, open-mouthed. Nobody ever stopped a class unless it was the teacher!

Danilova returned to the company as guest artist with Michael Maule, and joined us in Barcelona, remaining with us through the first part of our subsequent Royal Festival Hall season. She danced *Mademoiselle*, a bright, lightweight little ballet by Zachary Solov, and we wanted her to dance something else, so of course she repeated her famous Street Dancer in *Le Beau Danube*. The only time I ever danced the Golden Slave in *Schéhérazade* was with Danilova in Barcelona. During the pas de deux it began to appear that she was very nervous – so much so that at one point she completely forgot what she was doing, and I talked her through the rest of the pas de deux. Experienced artist that she is, nobody had the slightest idea that there was any crisis at all.

Chapter Seven

All that glisters is not gold, and some of Festival Ballet's seemingly more glamorous engagements turned out to be, in the event, highly uncomfortable. One of these was the fairy-tale wedding of Grace Kelly and Prince Rainier of Monaco, for which the company was invited to entertain.

We were naturally thrilled to be asked to Monaco. Dancers from several countries were also taking part, but the greater part of the entertainment was to be provided by the Paris Opera Ballet and Festival Ballet, with guest appearances by Margot Fonteyn and Michael Somes, and Tamara Toumanova. A great contingent of dance representatives from England and France descended upon Monte Carlo, which was also invaded by Americans and the world's press.

It all began well enough. The sun shone, the crowds were happy and excited, and we all went down to the harbour to see Miss Kelly's arrival. She had come from New York on the SS *Constitution*, which was of course too big to berth at the picturesque little port,and Prince Rainier went out in his yacht to bring his fiancée ashore. All the boats in the harbour, headed by the Onassis yacht *Christina* sounded their sirens, the band played, and there was the general hubbub of welcome. We saw the presentation bouquet, and craned our necks to see the film star who was soon to be princess, but all we saw was a large white hat, which effectively concealed her face.

The weather then saw fit to change. The rain began to fall and the temperature dropped . . . . and dropped. Not the ideal conditions for the open air performances which had been planned. Day after day there was a steady downpour, drumming on roofs and terraces – and still it grew steadily colder.

Palm trees dripped dismally and bunting hung limp and wet from the balconies. It became impossible to rehearse for the open air performance outside, and together with frustrated dancers the vast contingent of Miss Kelly's American relatives and guests was driven indoors. At the Hotel de Paris the regular guests, normally decorously in tune with its olde-worlde atmosphere, gazed in amazement at middle-aged women in Bermuda shorts, rampaging children tearing around firing off toy pistols, and loud-voiced men, accustomed to pitching their voices above the drone of air-conditioning. We began to realise that we were in for three days of hell – freezing to death at outdoor performances, so cold we could hardly move our limbs let alone dance. Then, by a miracle, the rain stopped in the nick of time, just when it seemed that everything would have to be cancelled. But there was no improvement in the temperature, which stayed relentlessly low.

The evening of 15th April was set aside for an open air rehearsal of the Serenade, to be given in the courtyard on the wedding eve, but as the rain fell unceasingly it became apparent that there was not the slightest chance of a rehearsal taking place. Next morning at 10.30, cold and depressed, newspapermen from all over the world gathered to see our first performance – a preview of the gala performance to be given on the night of the civil marriage. It seemed an ungodly hour at which to put on ballet. The weather had created an air of gloom, and the press members were just beginning to surface and shake off their hangovers. Margot Fonteyn and Michael Somes had not yet arrived from Finland, and the press sat somnolently through the Paris Opera's first offering, which was Lifar's *Divertissement à la Cour*. They – and we – warmed up considerably during our performance of *Etudes*, and everybody had relaxed to appreciate the *Pas de Quatre*. The performance ended with Festival Ballet's dress rehearsal of Michael Charnley's new ballet *Homage to a Princess*, which was well received.

The weather cleared by the eve of the wedding, and a huge stage had been set up in the Grimaldi Palace forecourt. It was still bitterly cold, and as there were no dressing rooms we had to change in the cells of the police station and then run for the stage. As if to add to our discomfort, everything was running late. Prince Rainier and Miss Kelly were to watch the performance from the palace balcony, but they were late in making their appearance, so thousands of people were trying to make the best of things as they waited patiently in the cold night air.

Folk songs and dances from Monaco were followed by the ballets, and Festival Ballet's contribution was a divertissement from *La Esmeralda* – the engagement scene in which the principal dancers were Belinda Wright, Marilyn Burr, Kenneth Melville and myself. Considering we had only had three hours' rehearsal it went remarkably well, and a splendid finish to the evening was in the form of a magnificent firework display in the harbour.

The Gala Performance in the Opera House on the night of wedding was a glittering affair. It was an occasion of pomp and circumstance, the auditorium scintillating with jewels and ablaze with gold braid gleaming on uniforms, splendid with all manner of medals and decorations. The programme was the same as that which the press had witnessed two days before, but with the addition of the 'Aurora Pas de Deux' danced by Fonteyn and Michael Somes. The programme was televised all over Europe as part of the Eurovision gala presentation. We were all invited to the reception and wedding breakfast, which was another spectacle of fairy-tale splendour, far outstripping anything which could have been devised on stage.

But we had to face one more trial by freezing the following night, when we had to repeat our theatre performance in the open air at the Louis II sports stadium. After any gala at the theatre there is a 'people's performance', so we were faced with a stage laid flat on a damp football field below the Rock of Monaco. The evening was bleak, with a bitter wind buffeting across the open space and nobody knew how to keep warm. The dressing rooms were a few hundred yards from the stage, and once again we risked pneumonia as we dashed about in our flimsy costumes. Despite the appalling conditions Margot and Michael Somes gave a magnificent 'Aurora Pas de Deux', and the audience loved every minute of the programme, which finished with Festival Ballet giving the dances from *Prince Igor*, together with the choir of the Monte Carlo Opera, and a background of tents, coloured smoke and fireworks.

It was indeed an exciting occasion, all of it, but will go down in my memory as one of the least comfortable dancing experiences of my career.

Probably the most rewarding country we visited was Israel – rewarding in the sense of overwhelming appreciation and enthusiasm. We went twice, in 1956 and 1958, and during the two year interval that wonderful young country accomplished so much that on our return the change was unbelievable. We were the first full scale ballet company ever to visit the Holy Land.

Even rehearsals aroused intense interest, and from the moment of our fantastic arrival, when the plane touched down at Tel Aviv airport on 2nd June 1956, we played to packed houses overflowing into the aisles. The Habimah Theatre, Tel Aviv, Israel's big national theatre, was decorated with British and Israeli flags, and our opening night was a full scale gala. Members of the Israeli Government attended, and the British Ambassador, Sir John Nicholls. We opened with *Napoli*, then went on to *Swan Lake*, Act II, the pas de deux from *Esmeralda* and *Prince Igor*.

We gave open-air performances at two Kibbutzin near the Sea of Galilee, so reminiscent of the New Testament stories, and all the biblical references seemed to come to life as we traversed the country via Nazareth. The facilities at the Kibbutzin were fairly primitive, but we didn't mind too much. There was no proper stage, no dressing-rooms, and the loos were in a tent, but the show went on!

Some performances were in a Roman amphitheatre, and never had *Swan Lake* and *Sylphides* looked more beautiful. My brother Tony, as stage manager, had to get up with the staff at 5 a.m. and go out to dig an orchestra pit for our conductor, Geoffrey Corbett, to stand in, as he was so tremendously tall.

Again the dressing rooms were primitive, and there were only two – one for the girls and one for the boys. Behind the stage a big backcloth was put up, and from the back of the arena could be seen the Hills of Jordan and the Sea of Galilee. At about 6.30 in those parts, a wind gets up, and when that happened the backcloth started flapping so violently that it had to be taken down again. The shutters were opened up so that they were end-on, and the audience could look right through to the Sea of Galilee. Then the moon came straight up over the hills until it looked as if moonlight and sea were flooding right across the stage. There was no scenery and none needed. It was a natural backcloth, and the most beautiful we had ever danced against.

With no curtains we used lights to dazzle the audience in order to make scene changes. The whole thing was a deeply emotional experience, with thousands thronging the vast area, and guards with rifles stationed all the way round the top tier because we were right on the border of Jordan!

In Haifa we danced in the Armond Theatre, a cinema with a terrible stage – we called it The Odeon. Then back we went to Tel Aviv with four days to rest, swim and sunbathe – apart from morning class of course. We met and made friends with a group of Yemenites called the Imbal Dancers. They were wonderful people who could trace their history right back to the Old Testament. They were air-lifted out of Yemen on the way to Israel. We all became great friends, and they invited us to parties, lighting fires to cook the food. And on the beach, under the stars, they put on a marvellous show of their folk dancing for us.

Our farewell performance was in the Ramat-Gan sports stadium, some miles out of Tel Aviv. Eighteen thousand people packed the arena, in the middle of which a temporary stage had been erected by the army, and under the supervision of Benn Toff. It was quite impossible to have scenery, but again thanks to Benn Toff, the army somehow procured enormous cypress trees and planted them behind the stadium. The army was invaluable, and supplied musicians and searchlights for the lighting. At dusk, as *Swan Lake* began, a full moon rose behind our transplanted cypress trees and made another magical setting for an unforgettable performance. It was not only memorable for the sheer beauty of its setting, but also for the thousands of flies, attracted by the powerful lights, which swarmed on to the stage and died. They became enmeshed in the girls' tutus and gave us all a most uncomfortable time. The last ballet was *Symphony for Fun*, and by that time the stage was so covered with dead and dying insects that we slipped uncontrollably on the treacherous surface, and some of us fell flat on our faces.

Dolin persuaded Markova to join us for our second visit to Israel in 1958. We had been invited to take part in the tenth anniversary celebrations of the State of Israel, and Israel very much wanted to see Markova dance. Once again we experienced the Israeli warmth, hospitality and enthusiasm. Great changes had been made since our first visit, and in Jerusalem we danced at the opening of a big new theatre and exhibition hall, The Mann Auditorium. This was the first building in what is now an enormous complex. We were the first foreign company to perform there.

My brother Tony had to leave for Jerusalem on the Friday night to get ready for Saturday's performance, travelling all the way by taxi. Sundown marked the start of the Sabbath and there was no public transport. When he arrived he found that the concert hall was still unfinished, there was no running water, and the place was so full of white dust that everybody would choke. But the show went on, and wherever Markova danced she received acclaim and adulation such as can have been given to few ballerinas anywhere in the world.

Dancing at a huge open-air stadium just outside Haifa we were again subjected to the most primitive of dressing-room accommodation. As if to make up for it, the audience was wonderful – 20,000 seats had been sold, and they were crowding into the aisles. Backstage we were struggling to dress. The corps de ballet's facilities were behind sets of screens, while the principals, including Markova, had tents. I shared a tent with Dolin, and towards evening was trying to organise myself for the performance. Tony was lying on the grass outside, waiting for the sun to go down and listening to my voice raised in loud lamentation that somebody had pinched the mat from our 'dressing room'.

What had happened was that Markova's sister, who cared for her like a mother hen, had removed it to Markova's tent. Suddenly the peaceful evening air was shattered by a wild scream, and Markova came flying out of her tent like a rabbit flushed from its burrow. She had found an enormous cockroach in the bucket provided as an improvised loo! While the commotion was going on, Tony, with great presence of mind, nipped into her tent, grabbed the disputed mat, and replaced it in our dressing room.

The performance was wonderful. Markova and Dolin danced *Giselle*, watched not only by the audience who had paid to get in, but also by crowds who thronged the surrounding slopes, and had a bird's eye view from blocks of flats and houses. For our farewell performance we were at Ramat-Gan arena in Tel Aviv, again to a capacity audience wild with enthusiasm. It was Markova's night. They adored her, and the stage was piled high with flowers as a continuous stream of bouquets was brought on to make a multi-coloured carpet. The audience shouted and re-called her again and again.

So our travels continued – so many personalities, so many memories. After Israel we made a long thirteen-hour overnight trip to Zurich, feeling very weary. All we wanted were baths, food and sleep, but the next day we were up and about early to begin *Nutcracker* rehearsals with the children from the Arts Educational Schools who had been flown out specially to take part. Our stage technicians worked for seventeen hours to prepare the stage of the Opera House for the first night of *Nutcracker*, and Zurich made us very welcome. Then it was on to Munich, Cannes, Nervi, and back to London . . . on we went, through the years and round the world. A happy company with a unique and wonderful spirit, from the highest star to the newest member of the corps de ballet, each determined to give the public the best they could offer, full of humour and enthusiasm.

All this was happening about a background of Julian Braunsweg's constant, just-losing battle with finances. The costs of new productions and the astronomic company travelling expenses meant a permanent shortage of cash. Julian went to unheard of lengths to procure funds, scheming, plotting, selling personal property and even his wife's jewellery in an effort to keep the company near enough solvent to carry on. It was a heroic struggle.

Being a ballet dancer has its drawbacks as does any profession, but the ballet is such a shut-in world, with time fully occupied by morning class, rehearsals and performances that it becomes like living in a convent. It is fatally easy to let one's range of interests be confined to the world of ballet; there is so little time to oneself. Fortunately for me, I love reading, and always had a passionate love of music. Even as a boy of seventeen, on my Australian tour, I dragged everywhere with me my case of heavy '78' type classical records. I never found too much difficulty in keeping in touch with the outside world, or so I thought at the time. It was only years later that I realised that perhaps I was wrong; I was more out of touch than I thought.

The constant tension of performing makes nerves continually taut, and dancers can't take relaxing pills because it is that very tension which makes a performance work. Male dancers also have to learn to build terrific strength. Few people realise that it takes as much if not more stamina to be a ballet dancer than an athlete . . . lifting all those ballerinas and making it look as if it's all so easy! All this of course means total dedication, which in turn means that anyone who has become a dancer must obviously be totally happy in what he or she is doing. It was my good fortune to be in that position.

I have always maintained that the arts can succeed in creating understanding when politicians fail dismally, and this was never more apparent than during Festival Ballet's sixteen-week tour of Europe in 1957.

Throughout my life in ballet there have been one or two landmarks in the form of truly memorable theatrical occasions. Our opening night at the Tivoli Concert Hall, Copenhagen, was one of these. Six years previously, Harald Lander, Ballet Master and Director of the Royal Danish Ballet, had been a victim of unpleasantness which had led him not only to renounce his position, but to leave Denmark completely. He went to the Paris Opera, and his second wife, Toni Lander, was Festival's prima ballerina in 1957, when we were due to visit Denmark.

Both Harald and Toni had been linked with the company for some years. Harald had choreographed *Napoli* for Festival Ballet in 1954, and his showpiece *Etudes* in 1955, but the Landers had not appeared professionally in their own country since leaving Copenhagen. It was Dame Adeline Genée who was greatly responsible for paving the way for their re-entry into the ballet world in their native country, and there was naturally some speculation as to how they would be received upon their return. Festival Ballet too was going to be on trial, our style inevitably to be compared with the Bournonville style of dancing.

Nerves were taut as we prepared for our opening performance, which began with Act II of *Nutcracker*. Dame Adeline Genée was in the audience, so too was the Danish Prime Minister and all the members of the Danish ballet company. Our second ballet was *Symphony for Fun* which I danced with Anita Landa, and then came *Etudes*, the Harald Lander ballet in which Toni Lander had the principal ballerina role.

Etudes is a ballet in which the excitement builds. It is a virtuoso exercise like a fireworks display, sprays of sparks leading eventually to an explosion of sound and activity. We had already taken several curtain calls for our previous ballets, but at the end of *Etudes* the house erupted. The orchestra paid us its own compliment in the form of a series of fortissimo chords, which punctuated the cheers and applause. Bouquets of flowers and laurel wreaths were thrown and carried on stage and placed at Toni Lander's feet, and it seemed the audience would never let us go. Anton Dolin made a speech and led Harald Lander on to the stage. His reception was phenomenal and the whole house rose to its feet. It was quite clear that anything which had been rotten in the state of Denmark in regard to the Landers was now forgotten, and they were welcomed back to their homeland in a blaze of glory.

At a supper party given that night for the company the Danish Prime Minister arrived unannounced and made a speech of welcome to the Landers, also congratulating Festival Ballet on a splendid performance.

Dame Adeline Genée reported to King Frederick upon the success of the evening, with the result that he telephoned the Tivoli to ask for seats for the following night. The box office naturally found tickets for him, and the story goes that he said he would 'go round and pick them up' – which apparently he did!

King Frederick received the Landers in the royal box after the performance, and Toni Lander was awarded the Knight Cross of the Order of Dannebrog, equivalent to our DBE.

So wedded was Festival Ballet to the traditional works that I was longing to dance something quite different.

It was perfectly understandable that Julian Braunsweg played safe with the box office classics. They always guaranteed an audience, and the company could not take risks. Its financial survival depended upon 'bottoms on seats', and if the seats were empty the company would die. A few new works had been introduced to the repertoire with varying results, but it was the classics which kept us afloat. However, when I visted Paris with Dolin I grew very excited about the possibilities of Festival Ballet staging Jack Carter's ballet *Witch Boy*, which seemed to me to have everything in the way of both dance and drama.

Adapted from the play *Dark of the Moon*, based on the American legend of Barbara Allen, Carter had first mounted it in Holland for the Netherlands Ballet. Norman McDowell had designed the costumes and sets and first danced the title role himself. I thought that not only would it enhance the repertoire of Festival Ballet, but it would also give another dimension to my own work if I had the opportunity to dance the role of the tragic, supernatural Witch Boy.

When Julian Braunsweg was offered the ballet for Festival, he was not at all convinced it would be a good idea. We had done nothing like it before, and as a businessman he asked for time to make up his mind. Such a venture could not be rushed. In fact, he took so long to consider the pros and cons that Jack Carter eventually threatened to give it to another company if he did not make a speedy decision.

I too was growing impatient. It was a long time since I had been so excited about a work, and I was anxious to know whether or not the coveted role would be coming my way. But Julian was not to be rushed.

'The sets are dismal!' he announced when he first saw the designs. 'The costumes are all too dark and not pretty enough. I must have time to think about it.'

He postponed his final decision yet again, and it looked as though he was going to veto the whole production. I saw my hopes of dancing Witch Boy fading rapidly, and my frustration eventually boiled over into anger. How much longer was I going to be confined to box office ballets? Both Dolin and I were convinced *Witch Boy* would be a success, and for the first and only time during my years with Festival Ballet I issued an ultimatum. I told Julian that if he decided against doing the ballet I would leave the company and work elsewhere. Whether it was as a result of this threat or a combination of pressures, Julian agreed that it should go into production. His own story is that he discovered it could be done for as little as £1,500 – a fact which helped considerably!

So rehearsals began, and we opened at Manchester Palace Theatre on 27th November 1957, with me in the title role as I had always hoped, and Anita Landa as Barbara Allen. My instincts as to its success proved entirely justified, and our first night received a tremendous ovation, with subsequent glowing reviews from the ballet critics. From that moment the future of *Witch Boy* was secure in the repertoire and it became one of my favourite roles.

The ballet's quality of 'other worldliness' and the sheer drama of the whole piece, in which Barbara Allen dies for her love of the Witch

Boy, who is lynched and then re-born, made it the most satisfying part I had ever danced. It was particularly well received in our tours of Italy and Spain, where audiences lap up any entertainment involving heavy tragedy or the supernatural.

Chapter Eight

In 1957 we toured Germany and Holland, and then went back to Paris where we gave a second season at the Théâtre Champs Elysées. While we were there David Lichine reproduced the Strauss romp *Graduation Ball*. This is based on the somewhat thin plot of an end of year ball at a girls' school, attended by a group of military cadets, invited as partners for the adolescent pupils. One of the show-pieces is the dance of the young drummer, which I danced at one time. It was a role in which I never fèlt quite right, and critic Clive Barnes was apparently not happy at my performance.

'John Gilpin was so wildly miscast,' he wrote, 'that common humanity restricts me to saying that he made a good entrance.'

Graduation Ball was an extremely good ballet. I had seen Nicholas Orloff in the role of the drummer when the de Basil Company did its last season at Covent Garden, and to this day I have never seen anyone to surpass him. I later danced the role of the leading cadet, which suited me better. It was the role created by Lichine himself, and was later danced in Festival Ballet by Keith Beckett, now a producer with Thames Television. He was superb.

We were scheduled to do *Etudes* during that Paris season, but as it was already in the repertoire of the Paris Opera permission was refused until there was a last minute intervention by Ambassador Sir Gladwyn Jebb. A distinguished guest at one of our Paris dress rehearsals was the great artist and designer Alexandre Benois.

Benois was another link with the historic days of Diaghilev. He came from a family of artists, writers and musicians, and was the great-uncle of actor Peter Ustinov. Benois had directed plays for the Moscow Arts Theatre, but he came into his own after meeting Diaghilev and turned his artistic genius towards the ballet. He designed the set for the original production of *Petrouchka*, and with his musical knowledge and imagination created the story of *Schéhérazade*

ight) In front of the church St Maria del Salute during y first visit to Venice, ımmer 1950.

elow) Rehearsing the *smeralda pas de deux* with arilyn Burr for the Ed ıllivan Show in the Qeluz alace, Lisbon, 1958. (Ed ıllivan in background).

At Noel Coward's home, Blue Harbour, Jamica, 1958. Left to right: Me, Noel Coward, Anton Dolin, Graham Payn, Alec Guinness.

With Her Serene Highness, the Princess Antoinette of Monaco, Theatre de Champs Elysees, Paris, 1957.

to Rimsky-Korsakov's music, which had not originally been written as an Arabian Nights theme.

And there was the great man at our dress rehearsal, aged eighty-seven – a lovely old gentleman with snowy white hair. He made an agreement with Julian Braunsweg to co-operate with a new production of *Nutcracker*, having already done a production for La Scala, Milan. I think that was probably our most successful version of the ballet, and certainly it is the production most people remember, even to this day. It was very simple, full of magic, and absolutely right for a children's ballet. We did a preview on 23rd December at the Royal Festival Hall for an audience of Dr Barnardo's children, which was a huge success.

Markova's sister persuaded her to return to the company for the Théâtre des Nations Festival at the Sarah Bernhardt Theatre in Paris. Festival Ballet was the dance company chosen to represent Britain, which was a great honour for us, and we were in the distinguished company of Glyndebourne Opera and the Old Vic.

When the company was on holiday at Christmas time I went to New York. The plane arrived during a snowstorm, and after spending five hours circling the airport we landed in a snowdrift. It was bitterly cold, as New York can be, and I spent most of the time dashing in and out of shops in order to avoid the icy winds and keep myself warm. Patrick was in New York too, visiting friends, and out of the blue one day he said, 'Noël wants to do a ballet for you. Would you like to go to Jamaica and talk about it?'

Needless to say this was one occasion when I did not hesitate about joining in yet another of Patrick's impromptu jaunts. We made the arrangements with true Dolin rapidity, set off for Jamaica to see The Master, and spent two weeks with him. A car was there to meet us at the airport, and after the chauffeur had driven us the seventy miles to Noël's house, Blue Harbour on the north shore, he promptly turned the car round and returned to the airport to collect Alec Guinness and his wife, who were guests at the same time. Alec was filming *Our Man in Havana*, and other guests included Joyce Carey and Graham Payn. Noel had just finished writing his play *Waiting in the Wings*, and every evening he would read parts of it to us, perched in a high-backed chair, looking like a cross between a wise old vulture and a Chinese mandarin.

Conversations during those two weeks constantly sparkled as Noël and Alec Guinness pitted their wits against each other, exchanging repartee, each trying to top the last brilliant witticism. Yet despite his often caustic wit, for which he was noted, Noël had a surprisingly puritan streak, with a distaste for off-colour language or smutty conversation.

So from those days in the Jamaican sunshine emerged the beginnings of *London Morning* – Noël Coward's only ballet, composed for Festival Ballet's tenth anniversary season. He had expressed a wish that it should receive its first performance in London, the city which inspired it, but in fact it was first performed in Lausanne, and came to London later. Jack Carter did the choreography and the costumes were designed by Norman McDowell. The decor by William Constable depicted a scene outside Buckingham Palace gates. The characters were tourists, city businessmen, guardsmen, a group of girls, a policeman, and a British sailor on leave, which was my role. Noël joined us for the first rehearsals in Barcelona, where my mother and her sister were staying. My aunt was very ill and had only a short time to live, so I brought them to Barcelona for a holiday. Noël was extremely fond of my mother, and she had admired him from afar since she was a girl.

I had been to Spain many times, but was amazed to learn that throughout his many travels Noël had never been there before. He was anxious to be shown around, and one weekend he suddenly said, 'Come on John. Where shall we go?' At that time we were in Madrid, and he was obviously keen to get away for the weekend and do some sightseeing. On many occasions during my life I have simply taken off without telling anybody and gone to see places simply because I love looking around by myself. It is part of my wanderlust and my restlessness and impatience – the latter mainly with myself. When Noël suggested the trip, the idea appealed to me enormously.

I always have a longing to get away, then when I have done what I want to do, I have to go on to something new. Maybe it's my Aquarian perversity.

Whenever I think of Noël I will always remember the two of us dashing off like rather naughty schoolboys, I as his guide, while we took in the sights and ate and drank ourselves silly. It was a delight to get to know him as a companion and confidant. Without telling a soul we hired a car and set off, going first to Segovia, then seeing the beautiful Roman aqueduct and Avila, one of Spain's lovely mediaeval walled cities, magnificently preserved, and the home of Saint Thérèse of Avila. Later I was with him on several occasions in Jamaica and Switzerland, and it was always a pleasure to be in the company of this kind, multi-talented man. He taught me many things which I have always tried to remember. One instruction was always to speak slowly and clearly, and another was to remember that an artist's exit from the stage door is as important as his bows on stage. A wonderful person to have known, and I feel very privileged to have been one of his friends.

Our 'lost weekend' in Spain was a marvellous experience, and being with Noël was always the greatest fun. He would talk to anybody, and if there happened to be a piano around he would always sit down and play. We arrived back from our jaunt to be greeted by the chorus of dismay which always met me on my return from my spontaneous trips . . . 'Where have you been? We were worried about you. Why didn't you say where you were going?'

Despite his charming manners at rehearsals Noël was a perfectionist, and his instructions as to how he wanted things done were very precise.

When he joined us for final rehearsals in Lausanne for *London Morning* there were moments when he – and indeed the rest of the company – wondered if the whole thing was going to come together in time for the first performance. Julian Braunsweg was having the costumes made by the proverbial 'little tailor round the corner', nothing seemed to be ready, and it was all completely chaotic. We were amazed and impressed by Noël's sheer professionalism; he didn't miss a thing, and his attention was everywhere. At the Festival Theatre one of the lighting gelatines was slightly the wrong shade. My brother Tony had already ordered a replacement, but Noël noticed the discrepancy immediately and remarked upon it.

'See that it doesn't happen again,' he added quietly, and one knew that it simply must never happen again.

After the last night in Lausanne the stage staff worked to the point of exhaustion until 2 a.m. to get the scenery and costumes down the hill to the station. There was only one café open at that hour, and all the members of the company were in evening dress, having an after-the-show party when Tony and the carpenters arrived. No evening dress for them. They were in their working clothes, dirty and tired. They flopped wearily at one of the tables outside and ordered themselves some drinks. After a short time Noël went out and joined them, chatting companionably. He was soon missed from the main party and Dolin went out in search of him.

'What are you doing out here?' he asked curiously.

'I'm sitting with my friends,' came Noël's prompt and laconic reply.

Now, so many years later, in the summer of 1981, I have just finished performing *Oh Coward* in Newfoundland, a show based on Noël's best known songs. I often thought of what he had taught me, and hoped he would have approved of my performances.

After the end of our run in Glasgow in March 1958, Louis Godfrey, Michael Hogan, André Prokovsky and myself, together with Anton Dolin, left for New York where we had been invited to appear on television on the Ed Sullivan Show. Dolin was to talk about his ballet *Variations for Four*, which had been produced for the Festival Ballet Birthday Gala the previous year, and we were to give a performance of it. *Variations for Four* lasts about eleven minutes, and as the Press got hold of the fact that the fee for our entire appearance on the Ed Sullivan Show was 11,000 dollars, much play was made of 'the ballet that costs a thousand dollars a minute'. The bandying about of such misleading phrases must have had a terrible effect on Julian Braunsweg's blood pressure because he, poor man, always had the greatest difficulty in keeping Festival Ballet's body and soul together!

The company had a great success in Paris that year, and Braunsweg had the brilliant idea of inviting the English critics to cross the Channel to our first night. It must have been the first time in British ballet history that they had been invited as a group to an English opening night on foreign soil. Dr and Mrs Braunsweg entertained them to dinner, after which they joined the glittering audience at the Théâtre Sarah Bernhardt. The theatre was in the throes of its annual festival during which dance and drama companies from all over the world perform.

In addition to the critics, French dancers turned out in force to see us. Fourteen ambassadors and their ladies took their seats in the intimate, packed auditorium. So too did Yves St Laurent, Charlie Chaplin and his wife, and representatives from all the arts. Markova and Dolin opened the programme with *Giselle*, which was well received – as indeed was the entire performance. The English critics made it clear that their trip across the Channel had been worthwhile. It was always Braunsweg's policy to 'send ze customers away 'appy,' and to that end he sent the Parisians away reeling from the heady draught of the bubbling *Etudes*. He always insisted that ballet programmes should be served to people with the same thoughtfulness with which one would plan a good meal – first the Hors d'oeuvre, then the pièce de résistance, and finally an easily digestible dessert. This was the formula upon which he always planned a triple bill.

It was a particularly exciting evening for us on stage, but unfortunately it was marred by an injury. Some stages are hard and difficult, which is why so many ballet injuries occur. This time it was not the stage which was responsible; no complaint could have been made about that. This was simply a tragedy which might have occurred anywhere.

In the Coda, towards the end of *Etudes*, the corps de ballet is all on stage, and there are three big entrances for the principals – on that occasion Flemming Flindt, myself, then the ballerina Toni Lander. All had been going beautifully up to that point. Flemming made his grand jeté entrance right across the stage, and suddenly there was a crack like a revolver. Seconds later Flemming was rolling on the floor in agony. The audience let out a shocked gasp, and with great presence of mind one of the other dancers, Michael Hogan, stepped in as Flemming was being carried off. I went on immediately afterwards and we finished the ballet without Flemming, who had snapped a tendon in his thigh, an injury which kept him away from dancing for about a year. At the end of the ballet Dolin and I carried him to Markova's dressing room (which used to be Sarah Bernhardt's), where he was made as comfortable as possible to await the arrival of a doctor.

Later that evening that same dressing room was invaded by what seemed like the whole of Paris, and, crammed like sardines amid the mountains of bouquets, we enjoyed a champagne supper, slightly saddened by Flemming Flindt's tragic accident.

In July we went to Nervi in Italy to take part in their International Festival of Dance, which was being held for the fourth year. We had been to Southern Europe and Israel, and by the time we reached Nervi our complexions were all in a state of advanced sun tan, with the result that one critic referred to 'the all-Negro cast appearing in *Les Sylphides* on opening night.' Performances at Nervi were in the open air, and *Sylphides* was particularly beautiful with the backcloth of trees and parkland. Paddy Stone, the Canadian dancer and choreographer, came to Nervi to create a new ballet for Festival Ballet, and it was certainly Something Completely Different. Northern Italy was at that time basking in one of its heatwaves, and Paddy Stone was a relentless workaholic. The four couples taking part in his new ballet, including myself and my partner Anita Landa, were literally worked until we dropped. The open air rehearsals were bad enough, but indoors the heat became quite impossible. The style of Paddy Stone's choreography was modern, based on South American rhythms of the Beguine, Fandango, Tango, Cha-cha-cha, Rumba and Samba. Arthur Wilkinson did the orchestration.

The ballet was not without its crises, and as nobody approved of the costumes they all had to be completely re-designed by Tom Lingwood. The ballet had been called *Classico* in Canada, but for us it was to be *Octetto*. It was slick and fun, and I enjoyed my solo, which was the Cha-cha-cha. It was a solo which stood up well by itself, and I included it in my 1960 programme in a concert tour of South Africa. I am still amazed at the number of people who seem to remember me in that particular dance.

Two months later, in September 1958, this ballet tortuously born under a blistering Italian sun was brought to the Royal Festival Hall. For some reason the title was thought to be unsatisfactory so there was a form of competition in which the audience was invited to find a new title. It was therefore initially advertised simply as 'The New Ballet', but as far as I know it was never re-christened, and *Octetto* it remained. It was not well received at Festival Hall on the opening night. Gracie Fields, who was our guest of honour that night, came on stage after the show and announced she had thought of a new title for the ballet – *Hot Pot*. This was a gift for a hostile critic, who wrote: 'The most apt title would have been to add 'ch' to both words!'

It was in 1958 that Serge Lifar and the Paris Opera originated the

Nijinsky Award – or the Prix Vaslav Nijinsky, as it was called – and I had the honour of being the first dancer to receive it. There was a certificate from Lifar and the Paris Opera, and there was to have been a statuette to go with it. I never received the statuette because they did not manage to get enough money together to have one cast!

Our first English performance of Noël Coward's *London Morning* took place at the Royal Festival Hall on 14th July 1959 and was very successful. There was such a demand for tickets during that summer season that we had to give twice as many performances of the ballet than were originally intended.

There were three great Giselles during the season – Markova, who danced with Vladimir Skouratoff as Albrecht, Chauviré partnered by Dolin, and Carla Fracci, who was dancing her first Giselle with me.

Yvette Chauviré was the greatest ballerina of France and of the French school of dance; she brought with her all her native characteristics of elegance and chic. We have an English style, which is very understated and far more disciplined than the French. English dancers have good legs and feet, and excellent line and lyricism, to me the most important factor of the dance. The American style has tremendous energy and can be said to have been almost entirely influenced by Balanchine, Robbins and Agnes de Mille.

I was a victim of Yvette Chauviré's French speed in 1952. My nose had been crooked ever since! We were in the middle of the pas de deux of *Nutcracker* Act II, and as Yvette prepared to do a pirouette she took off and caught me with her elbow across the bridge of my nose. Whether it was actually broken or not I have no idea, but it began to bleed copiously. I could not get offstage to stop the bleeding until we had finished the pas de deux, and there was great consternation from the audience as the blood poured down my face, looking very dramatic and more in keeping with a boxing champion than a Nutcracker Prince. Ever since that day I have a 'dent' in my nose, which is now slightly crooked.

Another award came my way in August 1959 in the form of one of the Anton Dolin Awards, which Dolin inaugurated to pay his own tribute to those who had made valuable contributions to ballet.

Sir Frederick Ashton (then plain Mr Ashton) of the Royal Ballet received the award for choreography, Nadia Nerina was the recipient of the ballerina award, and I was nominated for the award for the male dancer. The awards, which were statuettes of Dolin, were presented by Princess Antoinette of Monaco at a big ballet exhibition then on show at the Army and Navy Stores in London. Princess Antoinette is a great ballet lover, and during her stay in London came to see *Giselle* and *London Morning* with her children before leaving for a holiday in Scotland.

Despite my appreciation of the honour bestowed upon me in the form of the Dolin Award, my family was not so easily impressed. I left it with my mother while I went abroad, and when I came back she was irreverently using it as a doorstop!

There was much speculation at the end of 1958 and beginning of 1959 as to whether I would remain with Festival Ballet. On 25th February Julian Braunsweg put an end to the doubts by issuing a press statement to the effect that I had signed a two-year contract with Festival Ballet as premier danseur and Assistant Artistic Director. The latter was a fortuitous appointment as it turned out, because Dolin had a run of ill health later that year and I temporarily took over his position as Artistic Director of Festival Ballet. He was recovering from an attack of jaundice during the summer, and had gone to stay at his villa in Monte Carlo. At the end of August, after the Festival Hall season ended I too set off for Monte Carlo for my holiday, to join him at the villa.

Anxious to reach my destination as quickly as possible I drove all night and arrived exhausted at five o'clock in the evening. Patrick had been having some building works done, and a modern bath installed. In the guest bathroom was a magnificent Roman bath – a genuine article – very big, wide and long. It was made of marble and took an eternity to fill, so he had decided to have it replaced. In order to remove the huge structure the builders had to cut it in half. The villa was perched on a cliff, and the builders had to use a crane to lower the bath out of the house, after which it had to be lowered on to the road. It was halfway through its journey, and was leaning against the balcony which encircles the villa. The workmen were to complete the removal next day.

Patrick seemed to be very busy, rushing about as usual. I, on the other hand, was not capable of rushing anywhere after my long journey, and was sitting quietly in the living room when I heard a terrific crash and a groan. A few minutes later Patrick staggered in through the window from the balcony and almost fainted into a chair. He looked deathly pale.

'My foot!' he moaned in anguish.

Even though he was wearing leather shoes and black socks I could see a tremendous gash across his foot. For a split second I did not know what to do, as he was in obvious agony and a state of shock. A heavy section of the bath, propped up against the balcony, had fallen over and crushed his foot. There was blood everywhere, which I managed to staunch with towels, but he was in intense pain and it was essential to get medical help as quickly as possible. Unfortunately it was a Sunday, and almost impossible to get hold of a doctor.

The first person I thought of as a potential helper was Princess Antoinette, who lived in Eze. I telephoned her immediately and asked if she could alert her doctor and perhaps get Patrick into the Princess Grace Hospital. After an hour and a half, which seemed like an eternity, her doctor arrived. He gave a morphine injection and examined Patrick's foot. His big toe was mangled and two other toes were broken. The foot was wrapped, and the doctor said he would come back next morning. Between us, we managed to get Patrick upstairs and into bed, heavily bandaged and sedated.

At about four in the morning I was awakened by agonised moans coming from his bedroom next door. I went in to find him in terrible pain and the bedclothes covered in blood. The morphine had worn off, and it was obvious that the dressing had been hopelessly inadequate to hold back the bleeding. I felt desperate and at a complete loss to know what to do when I suddenly remembered two friends, John and Marjorie Etlinger, who were staying at a hotel in Monte Carlo. I telephoned them, and John came immediately. After a further phone call to the Princess Grace Hospital we were able to have Patrick admitted.

The damage to his foot was very serious, and he could not dance for some time. Six months later his toe joint had stiffened, requiring an operation in a Danish clinic by the 'dancer's saviour', Professor Eivend Tomassen, who told Patrick later that he was concerned that he could have had to lose his foot. That injury was sadly contributory to the demise of Patrick's career as a performer, although it in no way hampered his subsequent activities of directing, teaching and acting. Today he is doing more than ever.

As temporary Artistic Director I was dancing most nights and taking classes and rehearsals by day, which was exhausting, and somehow I did not have Patrick's ability to do a thousand things at once.

There had long been hopes that Festival Ballet would one day pay a visit to South America, but finances had never permitted such a trip until the beginning of 1960. With the sponsorship of the British Council, together with additional aid from Shell and Rolls Royce, well established in South America, it was possible to go ahead. The tour was to last for eleven weeks, and was to be the first visit to Latin America by a British ballet company. We were to cover seven countries in the course of the visit, performing in Mexico (Mexico City), Venezuela (Caracas), Colombia (Bogota), Peru (Lima), Chile (Santiago), Brazil (Sao Paulo and Rio de Janeiro) and Argentina (Buenos Aires).

The British Council gave a cocktail party for the company before we left, and there was great excitement among the dancers at the proposed tour. I had been suffering from a certain amount of back trouble after the fall I had at the Drury Lane Gala in November 1959, but I was in good form and was sure I would be up to the demands of the tour. Dolin was also back to his old form after the accident to his foot during the summer, and apart from fitting in inoculations between performances, we were all set to go. We left London Airport on 11th March and flew to Mexico City. There were sixty-four in the company and somehow four tons of costumes, props and scenery for the sixteen ballets we were to perform had also got to be transported. The usual containers were too large and heavy to be carried by air, so special modifications were made and lightweight fibre containers were specially manufactured.

The opening performance was at the Belles Artes Theatre in Mexico City, and was such a success that we were asked to do extra performances in the University auditorium, seating 16,000.

Although we were the first large British company to appear there, Mexico was no stranger to some of the world's greatest dancers. Everyone seemed to remember the 1947 ballet season, when Markova and Dolin, with Ballet Theatre, danced in the same programme as the Mexican Ballet. Our first night audience was no doubt recalling that season, and they gave us a great welcome as we opened with Act II of *Swan Lake*, followed by *London Morning* and *Etudes*. After arriving in Mexico City we only had three days before giving our first performance, but clearly that was not long enough in which to get used to the altitude. There were oxygen cylinders in the wings, and we found ourselves gasping for breath and having to gulp in oxygen before returning to the stage. Some dancers actually fainted, and during *Swan Lake* on that first night we found it difficult to lift our arms and legs. Lungs full of inhaled oxygen made us extremely light-headed, and it was difficult to know which was worse! But nothing was quite so bad as the combination of high altitude and humidity which we encountered in Bogota. Everyone felt slightly sick, so the advice meted out to us was to eat only light food. Dancers are inclined to get hungry, and the result of our enforced diet meant that we all promptly lost weight.

South American hospitality was lavish, and we always seemed to be going to parties of one kind or another after evening performances. The 'mornings after' were thus rendered very uncomfortable. We travelled everywhere by chartered planes, which always left early in the mornings when we were at our most jaded. Getting on to an aeroplane at 7.30 a.m. was never a comfortable experience, even when the plane took off without a hitch, but the flight from Mexico City to Caracas was memorable for the apparent reluctance of the plane to leave the ground.

We duly esconced ourselves on the aircraft at 7.30 a.m., glumly hung over from the previous night's junketings, and took our seats. After a quarter of an hour we were asked to vacate the plane because an oil leak had been discovered in the brakes. We sat around for four hours, and were then told we could board the plane once more. By this time we all felt a bit better, so cheerfully fastened our seat belts and heard the engines start up. We could hardly believe it when we were once again asked to leave the plane. Another aircraft had crashed on the runway so there was no chance of leaving until it had been cleared. By this time our confidence in our chartered plane had been somewhat sapped, and as the heat of the day began to increase we sat around perspiring until 2.30, when another attempt was made to take off. Not only had the hot sun got to us, but it had also affected the plane! The petrol had overheated while the plane had been standing all those hours on the runway in a blistering sun, and there was no chance of a take-off until later.

Nerves jangling, we decided to go back to our hotel, where we later ordered dinner. Eventually, in the middle of dinner we were told to report back to the fated runway as we were taking off at 6.30, and we were all absolutely horrified to see that we were about to leave on the same jinxed aircraft. There seemed to be no chance of it ever reaching its destination without mishap if its day's record was anything to go by. Was Festival Ballet going to crash to oblivion, we wondered. And what about our evening performance? We were due to open in Caracas that night. Needless to say, the performance had to be cancelled as we did not arrive until 9 p.m., totally shattered by the day's events.

We gave an extra matinée to make up for the missed performance.

On we went in triumphant progress to Santiago, Sao Paulo, Rio and Buenos Aires where, at the Teatro Colon we took part in a gala performance to celebrate the 100th anniversary of the founding of the Republic of Argentina. On the same bill was the resident company of the Teatro Colon and the Marquis de Cuevas company. We danced *Etudes* at the end of the programme and received an ovation lasting over ten minutes. As a result of this success we did a television performance of *Etudes* before an invited audience.

My long friendship with Nancy Oakes started dramatically in South America. She is the daughter of the victim of one of the most famous unsolved murder mysteries of modern times, set in the Bahamas.

I was invited to one of her parties in Mexico City, and collapsed at the festivities, to all appearances looking as though I was dying. We had come up from sea level, and with no time to get acclimatised to the high altitude, plunged straight into a performance, helped out with whiffs of oxygen. I had danced just before the party, and apparently the extraordinary effort had taken more out of me than I realised.

Luckily for me, one of Mexico's leading doctors was one of Nancy's guests, so I was carried from the party and put to bed with expert attention. But Nancy was badly frightened, and told me afterwards that she had genuinely feared I was going to die.

Her house, in the old part of Mexico City, like so many Latin houses, had an anonymous facade from which a door opened to an interior like a film set. The foyer led straight on to a swimming pool, beyond which was the drawing-room. The Russian Ambassador was present at one of her parties, and I thought it might show courtesy to speak to him in Russian.

Accordingly, I asked Andre Prokovsky, one of the dancers in the company, how I should greet him.

'You should say,' began Andre . . . . . and he taught me a phrase in Russian. Overlooking the glint in his eye, I advanced upon the Ambassador, smiled ingratiatingly, and politely repeated the phrase. It was as though I had laid the foundations for the third world war. The poor man went quite white, and looked at me rather strangely. In a flash I remembered the gleam in Andre's eye, and realised what must have happened. I wished, in one split second that I could die (from embarrassment) and at the same time strangle Andre, because I found out later that I had charmingly said the Russian equivalent of 'You are a stupid fool!'

At the end of our South American tour we had travelled 25,000 miles and given fifty-seven performances in seventy-nine days. During our stay in Lima both Julian Braunsweg and Anton Dolin were honoured by the Peruvian Government in the form of the award of medals of the Order of the Sun of Peru, the country's highest honour.

Chapter Nine

In 1960 Nice was celebrating the centenary of the union of the Comte of Nice with the French Republic, and Serge Lifar choreographed *Bonaparte à Nice (1796)* specially for Festival Ballet to celebrate the event. He also did me the honour of choosing me to dance the role of the young Bonaparte. The music was by Maris Thiriet and the costumes by André Lavasseur, but after its French première the ballet was not a great success.

We first performed it in England at the Royal Festival Hall on 19th July, the opening night of our summer season. To put it mildly, it was not favoured by rave reviews. Clive Barnes, then critic for the magazine *Dance and Dancers*, stated that he was not sure whether or not it was intended to be a funny ballet. (It wasn't.) He obviously found it hilarious.

> 'It opens with a tableau featuring, I think, the young Napoleon surveying some somewhat assorted troops,' [he wrote].
>
> The troops amuse themselves playing leap-frog. Napoleon re-enters riding a white hobby-horse and careers around the stage as though he didn't mind a bit. The troops are rather impressed by this. They are even more impressed when he detaches himself from the hobby-horse and hurls himself into a classical variation . . . If nightmare memory serves, some girls come on also riding or wearing hobby-horses . . .

The tone of the critics can perhaps be deduced from this classic piece of satire.

Julian Braunsweg added the anecdote that the ballet had been put together so quickly, it was only discovered after the third performance that the fibre-glass hobby-horses so much in evidence, actually had no ears! *Bonaparte à Nice* had but a short life.

A month after Festival Hall audiences were treated to the

adventures of the young Bonaparte, they were able to see our first performance of *Bourrée Fantasque*, the Balanchine ballet to Chabrier's music. Balanchine was unable to come to England to produce it himself, so he sent his ballet mistress Una Kai to reproduce it. This fared better than Bonaparte and has remained in the repertoire, but Braunsweg always maintained it was not good box office and had to be sandwiched between a *Sylphides* and a *Prince Igor* to make it palatable. For me it was a very fine work, and I only wished we had more Balanchine ballets in the repertoire. We did later add his *Night Shadow*.

I was beginning to feel the need to move on and give myself more scope as a dancer. I had been with Festival Ballet for ten years, and was thirty years old. Much as I loved the company and felt a great loyalty towards it, I could not entirely repress the instinctive wish to expand my dancing activities. Throughout the fifties I had made no guest appearances elsewhere because I was always needed at Festival Ballet. It was becoming increasingly obvious that Festival was going to have no money to risk on new untried ballets, and if I did not make a move then, when I was at my peak, I might lose chances which could come my way only by releasing myself from the company. It was essential that I make some changes, and that I made them without further delay.

Changes there were, both in my professional and my private life.

In August I married Sally Judd, a member of the corps de ballet in Festival Ballet. The wedding was a full scale production at St Mary's Church in the Boltons, Kensington. All our family and friends came, and the guest list read like a Festival Ballet Who's Who, headed of course by Markova and Dolin. It has always been a sore point with Patrick that when Julian Braunsweg wrote his book, he indicated that because Patrick did not approve of the marriage he did not attend the ceremony.

'The whole company was at the wedding a few months later,' he wrote. 'There was one notable exception – Dolin.'

This is quite untrue, and perhaps now is the time to set the record straight. Dolin was most certainly there, escorting Princess Antoinette of Monaco, whom we were honoured to have among our guests.

It was a magnificent occasion, but in how many cases do these wonderful wedding days lead to eventual sadness and partings? It seems impossible, amid the euphoria of The Great Day, to contemplate that such fairy stories do not always have happy endings. Looking back, I ask myself why I married. I imagine at the time I was experiencing another need, another horizon. Perhaps I thought at last I would have someone who would love me for what I was as a person and not as an artist. In the beginning I had really wanted it to work, although it was a pretty stormy marriage at times.

It did not last. My art had to come first, and that took me away from home a great deal. I valued my so-called freedom and independence too dearly. I don't blame Sally – I think she realised she could not hold me or change me, but I like to think we gained and learned a little from our relationship. I believe she felt she could change me and be the one person to fulfil my needs. How could she have realised that I did not know – and still do not know to this day – what those needs really are.

Our daughter Tracy was born in 1962, and is now growing into a fine young lady. There are times when I feel guilty that I did not spend more time with her when she was growing up. As a baby and before she went to school she always had a nanny because Sally went back into the theatre and was very busy re-establishing her own career. Tracy then went to boarding school at a very early age, to my old school, the Arts Educational Schools. During the last two years she and I have seen more of each other, and seem to be growing closer at the same time as she is rapidly becoming an independent adult. Sally and I remain good friends, and she brought up Tracy very well, although I would like to think I had a small part in it. It is never easy for a child to accept divorce, and harder when a parent remarries, which Sally has done. Fortunately Tracy has become well adjusted to the situation. I hope in the future our relationship will remain close.

At the end of the Festival Hall summer season in 1960 Sally and I left Festival Ballet, and in September Anton Dolin, Belinda Wright, Toby Fine from the Cape Town Ballet, and myself, set off for an eight-week tour of South Africa to give a series of concert performances. Sally came too, and it was by way of being a honeymoon trip for us. The tour had been arranged by Toby Fine's husband, David Bloomberg, and as the group was not large enough

(*Right*) In front of 'The Gateway to India', Bombay, 1953.

(*Below*) Marina Svetlova, Anton Dolin, and me with Kathakali Dancers in Kandy, Ceylon, 1953.

(*Top*) On tour in the English provinces with Anton Dolin. (*Bottom*) *Homage to a Princess* the ballet produced for the wedding of Prince Rainier and Grace Kelly in Monte Carlo. L to R: Marilyn Burr, Belinda Wright, Michael Charnley, Anton Dolin, André Lavasseur, Anita Landa, Louis Godfrey. In front: Ronald Emblem and me.

(*Left*) Taking a stroll around Florence with Natalie Krassovska.

Sightseeing in Italy with my brother Tony, Daphne Dale and Noel Rossana of Festival Ballet.

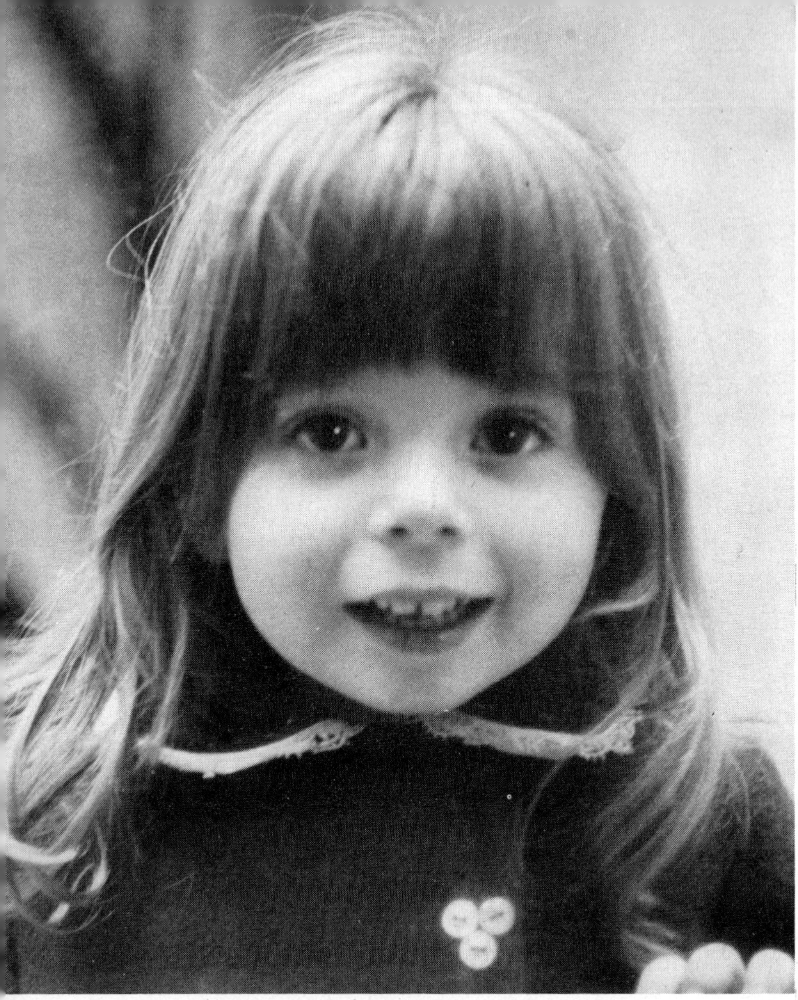

My daughter Tracy. An ea
portrait and (below) as sh
today.

to be termed a 'company' we travelled under the title of Celebrity Ballet. A ballet recital of this kind is really a series of concert performances, and more difficult and exacting to present than a full scale production. The limitations of not having a corps de ballet and large orchestra were overcome, and audiences did not seem to mind. With our two excellent pianists we opened in Cape Town to ecstatic reviews, followed by visits to Durban and Johannesburg.

I had visited Cape Town previously in 1949, when I was on my way back from Australia, although I had never danced there. I loved it, and found the whole of South Africa a beautiful place with a wonderful climate. It was in Cape Town that I first met author Mary Renault, whose books I always admire. We became great friends and still correspond with each other to this day.

For an English dancer Covent Garden is what the Bolshoi is to the Russians. While I was dancing with Carla Fracci in Milan I received a cable from Ninette de Valois, asking if I would be available to dance in the Spring season at Covent Garden. This was an opportunity not to be missed, and I was delighted to accept. In terms of experience and international reputation I had come a long way since 1949, when I had approached Ninette about joining Sadlers-Wells. Because of the opportunities afforded for travel with Festival Ballet my work was well known throughout the world, Indeed, I often thought it a strange quirk of fate that I had received more recognition abroad than in my own country. Not that I was ungrateful; I had had a wonderful time. Rambert had helped to create me, Festival Ballet had made me what journalists are pleased to call 'a star', and the accolades had come my way. Now, to my great delight, I had the summons to the Royal Opera House, Covent Garden, to join as permanent guest artist.

My debut there was on 18th April 1961 as The Blue Boy in *Les Patineurs,* a role originally created by Harold Turner in 1937. Sir Frederick Ashton's choreography ingeniously suggested that the dancers were skating. There was no story, except that it was a comment upon a skating party, with the various personalities disporting themselves on the ice to music by Meyerbeer, which had been arranged by that great ballet musician Constant Lambert.

The role of The Blue Boy was the 'show-off'. It was a technical virtuoso part, full of leaps and spins, and everyone thought I would be just right for it. I had some misgivings because I felt – and still feel – that it is perhaps for a demi-character dancer. I enjoyed it of course, but would have preferred to make my first appearance with the Royal Ballet at Covent Garden in *Giselle* or a classical role with which I was more familiar. Eventually I danced all the classical roles there, and did my very first full length *Sleeping Beauty* with Antoinette Sibley, with whom I loved dancing. It was an excellent partnership, although not as famous as her later partnership with Anthony Dowell. I also partnered Merle Park, Anya Linden, Lynn Seymour, and, of course, Margot Fonteyn.

Lynn Seymour is one of the truly great ballet stars, and certainly one of the finest dramatic ballerinas we have in this country today. She is a loner and a kind of rebel, and adds an unpredictable quality to any production, a factor I find lacking at Covent Garden today. Her unpredictability could of course have its disadvantages when partnering her, but the minute she came on stage everyone was aware that they were going to see something special. She was like a small puppy – one week she would put on weight, and the next week promptly take it off again. Her whole personality is up and down like a yo-yo, but she has always been outstanding within the ranks of the Royal Ballet, and now she is to lend her individuality to dancing of a different kind, away from the major companies.

The Royal Ballet boasts some excellent dancers, but somehow they are not exploited in the right way; it is all left too late. Audiences go to the ballet to see great stars, but it is a disadvantage of the present system that our dancers are not given their opportunities at the right time.

The state of dance in England at present is unexciting, and greatly in need of an injection. Like all arts it goes through bad patches, and perhaps this is one of them. Some outstanding dancers emerged in the sixties – the ballerinas already mentioned, and of course Anthony Dowell. The seventies were not so productive, although there have been some fine dancers and exciting new works, such as *A Month In The Country*. Marguerite Porter has enormous potential, but, again, is being left rather late, as she is already in her early thirties. I find it hard to call to mind anybody else outstanding. So much could be done with our dancers, but it is the fault of the system that they are not given their heads. Only Anthony Dowell, of the contemporary

English male dancers, is internationally known, and then only because he left the Royal Ballet to dance in the States. From my old company, Festival Ballet, there is nobody who stands out head and shoulders above the others, although I have great admiration for David Wall and Stephen Jefferies, both fine artists.

Partnerships are also important, and a great aspect of the star system. Throughout the history of the ballet there have been some memorable partnerships which have created exciting performances and contributed tremendously to the art. Going right back, there was the Nijinksy-Karsavina partnership, later there was Markova-Dolin, Fonteyn-Nureyev, Dowell-Sibley, and my own partnerships with Belinda Wright and Lucette Aldous.

At the beginning, I found my time at Covent Garden difficult. I had been used to dancing eight performances a week from the age of fifteen, and at the Royal Ballet I was only dancing about three times a month. For a dancer used to constant performing this was not easy. The gaps between performances made every one like an opening night.

No matter how much work a dancer does in a classroom, it is the work on stage which is so important, and I felt I was not on stage enough to maintain my dancing at its best. Of course I attended class each day, but on the occasions when I was to appear at Covent Garden it was like coming out of cold storage; I missed the constant stimulus every day of knowing I had a performance. I asked Ninette de Valois if I could join the touring company, which would give me more actual performances. She agreed, and so I found myself with more work to do, perhaps dancing at Covent Garden one night and somewhere like Liverpool the next, with the touring company, but I preferred to do that.

I danced *The Sleeping Beauty* in the provinces, but because of various mishaps I was never able to repeat it at Covent Garden, which was regrettable. I was still suffering from a certain amount of back trouble which kept recurring in a minor way, and on one occasion when I was due to dance *Sleeping Beauty* at Covent Garden with Lynn Seymour she had a knee injury, which meant a last minute change of plan. It seemed a strange quirk of fate that I had waited so long to join the Covent Garden company, but somehow I was not making the progress I had hoped for at that Mecca of the dance world. Things kept going wrong, and towards the end of 1961 Ninette had a message from Julian Braunsweg asking if I could go back to Festival Ballet to dance their Christmas *Nutcracker* season. Dolin had by that time left the company, and as there was no other potential *Nutcracker* Prince, I returned, remaining with Festival until 1972, through all their subsequent trials and tribulations.

Then comes the ultimate eternal question – did I make the wrong move, and should I have stayed with the Royal? Had I done so things might have changed for the better, but I am not one to believe in regrets. One does what seems right at the time, and I believe things are Fate ordained. For much of the time at Festival Ballet I felt frustrated because I knew that inside me there was much to give. Choreographers worked around my technical abilities. Nothing came up which really exploited my all-round capability until *Witch Boy,* and when I reflect upon it, it seems incredible that the international reputation I enjoyed was created on so few original works. There are many roles I would have loved to do, for example *L'Après Midi d'un Faun.* We had it in the Rambert repertoire when William Chappell danced it, but of course I was too young. I would have liked to dance the Prokofiev *Romeo and Juliet*, although I danced the Tchaikovsky version with Belinda Wright, choreographed by Oleg Briansky. I would also have liked to dance in *Daphnis and Chloe*, but it was not to be.

While I was still with the Royal Ballet Margot Fonteyn arranged her Gala for the Royal Academy of Dancing, to be given at Drury Lane on 2nd November 1961. Nureyev's defection to the West was much in the news at that time, and he expressed the wish to dance at the Gala with Margot. Many critics had compared him with Nijinsky, and he wanted to dance *Spectre*, but Margot told him she was already dancing it with me at the Gala. He made his first London appearance dancing magnificently with Rosella Hightower the Black Swan pas de deux, and a special solo choreographed for him by Sir Frederick Ashton.

For me that was a very special performance of *Spectre*. We were coached for ten days by the great Tamara Karsavina, who created the role of the young girl, and danced it with Nijinsky. It was a great privilege to work with her. She naturally concentrated a great deal on Margot's performance, but it was wonderful to watch, and I learned so much during that time. The most marvellous feature about Karsavina was her eyes, and the incredible atmosphere she could create during the ballet. Many male dancers think of the Nijinsky role as a great athletic feat, but *Spectre* is like a jewel box. The role of the spectre is not easy in that it has to be merely a perfume – not male, not female, but the essence of the rose. How lucky I am to have worked with such people as Karsavina, who was able to explain the original intention behind the ballet when first produced in 1911.

She had been to Festival Hall in August 1954 when we gave a special performance to commemorate the 25th anniversary of Diaghilev's death. I was dancing *Spectre* with Anita Landa on that occasion, and Karsavina had coached her in the role. When the curtain rose that night Karsavina was revealed standing by the window in the famous setting. She came down to the footlights to speak to the audience of the first performance of the ballet, and about the days with Diaghilev, creating a spell-binding atmosphere before Anita and I took over in the Nijinsky-Karsavina roles. It was one of those occasions when one realises the particular magic of ballet tradition, handed down through the generations of great dancers. So little was written down in those early days, and it is invaluable to have had such artists as Karsavina who had bridged the gaps with first-hand knowledge.

It is always difficult in Great Britain to find money to subsidise the arts, and even a major company like Festival Ballet constantly suffered from a lack of funds, even though it always looked so prosperous.

In 1962 it was decided that a Trust should be formed, and Festival Ballet Ltd. went into liquidation. Julian Braunsweg's statement of the situation which was issued at the time, shows the tremendous struggle which was put up to keep the company solvent and able to continue to perform:

> It is with very great sorrow that the Directors of Festival Ballet Ltd. have had to convene a meeting of its creditors with a view to the company being placed in liquidation. I am determined, however, that the London Festival Ballet, which has contributed so much to ballet in this country, shall continue its existence.

One thing has been proved to me beyond any doubt. It is that my sincere attempt to run a ballet company without a substantial subsidy or grant is hopeless. I am, however, thankful that I managed to build up the reputation and the artistic accomplishments of the London Festival Ballet over the past thirteen years. Apart from two annual seasons at the Royal Festival Hall, at Christmas and during the summer when the company plays to audiences totalling over 230,000 each year, we have paid regular visits to the provinces and have undertaken very extensive foreign tours. In fact, we have become known as 'the world's most travelled company'. Tribute has been paid by British diplomatic representatives wherever we have gone to the good relations which we have fostered with foreign countries as a result of these tours. Unfortunately all these things do not make an artistic company financially secure.

Some creditors have shown us the utmost forbearance but others have precipitated a position which has made it inevitable for the London Festival Ballet Ltd. to go into liquidation. A decision has been taken, however, immediately to set up a non-profit-making concern which will be known as the London Festival Ballet Trust Ltd.

On this new basis we shall apply for financial grants and aids from Local Authorities, the Arts Council, cultural foundations, commercial concerns and indeed from members of the public. The ballet company as such will go on, and they and I will always be grateful for the loyal support which the public has given us in the past and which we are sure will be extended to us in the future.

The new non-profit making concern of London Festival Ballet Trust Ltd. which is now in the course of incorporation will be carrying out the engagements already announced, followed by a proposed European Tour of 6 weeks Italy, 4 weeks France, 3 weeks Switzerland, 3 weeks Germany.

JULIAN BRAUNSWEG
Director General
London's Festival Ballet.

Chapter Ten

The financial obstacles besetting Festival Ballet continued, and somehow Julian Braunsweg continued to surmount them and still produce new ballets for the repertoire. In 1963 one of the major works mounted was *Peer Gynt* to the Greig music, choreographed by Vaslav Orlikowsky.

A grant was forthcoming from the then London County Council to the tune of £10,000, but it was not enough. The production cost nearer £15,000 and the difference was made up by a gift of £4,000 from one of the Marks family (of Marks and Spencer). The ballet was given its premiere in Monte Carlo on 13th April 1963. I danced the title role, with Marilyn Burr, Irina Barowska, Olga Ferri and Irene Skorik in the leading female roles. During our tour of Europe we were to present *Peer Gynt* at the Opera House in Rome at a Gala Performance to celebrate the opening of the new Hilton Hotel there. At the last minute the Hilton management cancelled the event because the Pope had died. The company was stranded without the finances which would have been forthcoming from the Gala.

Braunsweg tried to persuade the Hilton management to pay the fee anyway, but they demurred, obviously indignant that he should be thinking of anything as mundane as money at a time of national bereavement. They eventually agreed to pay half the fee, and the London County Council sent money to Genoa as an advance on the Festival Hall takings, so we were able to proceed with the tour.

Talks were in progress concerning a possible merger between Ballet Rambert and Festival Ballet, but it was clearly not going to be feasible. The LCC said it was impossible to go on financing a company which had no Arts Council grant, and the Arts Council, which already subsidised Ballet Rambert, said it could not afford to offer assistance to a third major company. Festival Ballet was going to have to struggle along by itself.

Meanwhile, dancing was our business and we continued to dance. I was honoured to receive, in 1963, the Queen Elizabeth II Coronation Award for services to British Ballet. This was followed in 1964 by my winning the Etoile d'Or, the only English dancer to have done so. The award was for my performance in *Nutcracker* at the International Festival of Dance in Paris. I did not hear of my success until a couple of months later because the award is not made instantly, but when the whole season is over. I was told when we were dancing at the San Carlos in Naples, and had to travel to Paris to receive it. Galina Samsova, who had joined Festival Ballet at the beginning of 1964, had been the recipient of the award the previous year for her performance in *Cinderella* with the de Cuevas company, so she and I travelled to Paris together so that she could present the medal to the next winner – myself. It was thought that we would not reach Paris in time for the presentation, but by leaving Naples very early in the morning we made it in time. The British Ambassador had been alerted, and he was going to receive the award on my behalf, but happily I was there to receive it myself.

The Royal Festival Hall was in the midst of a re-building programme in 1963-64, so we were unable to perform on what had become our 'home ground'. Instead we did a season at the Royal Albert Hall, where we appeared with dancers from the Kirov and Bolshoi companies, and from Budapest and Helsinki State Operas. We gave our Christmas season that year at the New Victoria Theatre.

In early spring 1965 Lucia Chase, the founder and director of American Ballet Theatre, invited me to appear as guest during their 25th anniversary season at the State Theatre, in the Lincoln Centre in New York. Toni Lander was with the company, and her husband Harald was mounting *Etudes*, which I had already danced with Toni for Festival Ballet. It was very exciting for me to be dancing with Ballet Theatre for the first time a role I had created ten years previously.

Ballet Theatre had approached me to join them when I left de Cuevas in 1951, but I could not do so as I had already committed myself to Festival Ballet. So 1965 was the first time I had actually danced in New York – I had danced with Festival Ballet at the Brooklyn Academy, but the State Theatre was 'New York proper'. I was to appear in the opening performance, dancing *Etudes* with Toni Lander and Royes Fernandez.

I was slightly nervous, turning up for rehearsal on the first day as guest artist with a new company, and Toni Lander made a disclosure which did not add to my confidence. 'I've told them, John,' she said jokingly, 'that you are the only one who has ever done the full series of grands pirouettes without a stop, plus the fouettés. Nobody believes you can do it, so you must not let me down!' And there was the full company on the first day, all waiting for me to perform this particular feat, which fortunately went off without a hitch.

During that season I also danced Albrecht in *Giselle*, a unique occasion because Dolin brought the great Russian ballerina Olga Spessivtseva to the first performance. He had danced his first Albrecht with her in 1932 – indeed, she had taught him the role. Spessivtseva was a famous Aurora in the great *Sleeping Beauty* production at the Alhambra Theatre, and ballerina of the Paris Opera for many years.

Her later life had been a sad one. She had a breakdown and was in a mental hospital for nearly twenty years. It was Dolin who was responsible for getting her out – cured. That New York production of *Giselle* was her first visit to the ballet since she had been ill, and it was an extraordinary experience for me to be dancing for her on such an occasion. Dolin brought her round to my dressing room after the performance, and again there was that unreal sensation of having stepped back into the past history of the ballet. Spessivtseva – one of the magic names of the Russian ballet – and suddenly there she was in my dressing room. It was wonderful to meet her.

It was a very exciting season for me. I danced *Les Sylphides* and the famous *Esmeralda* second act pas de deux, which Beriosoff had mounted for Festival Ballet.

Julian Braunsweg had always found a means of rescuing Festival Ballet from recurring financial disasters, but in 1965 even the resourceful Julian was defeated by a costly production of *Swan Lake*.

We were unable to give our usual summer season at the Royal Festival Hall because a booking had already been accepted from the Bolshoi for a group of their dancers to appear. We therefore performed at the New Victoria cinema, owned by the Rank Organisation. Our season was to have lasted six weeks, during which there would be a new full length version of *Swan Lake* which Orlikovsky was to produce. Benn Toff, who had left the company in South America, returned to work for the great production, and the young Australian designer John Truscott, who had just designed *Camelot* for Drury Lane, Australia and Hollywood, was engaged to do the costumes.

The budget for the production was set at £20,000, but it was soon obvious this was not going to be nearly enough.

The designer had three months in which in which to complete his sets and costumes. He thought he would be hard pressed to have everything ready in time, so more hands had to be employed. Costs seemed to be mounting daily. Everyone was under tremendous pressure to be ready for the first night, so temperaments began to fly. Truscott and Orlikovsky had one row after another, Benn Toff went into hospital suffering from overwork, and Julian Braunsweg was out of his mind with worry – partly about finances, and partly because it seemed we would never make the deadline of opening night.

The costumes were continuing to arrive in all their magnificence, each one more elaborate and expensive than the last. Truscott refused to compromise or economise, and everything had to be real. My own costume for Act III was a masterpiece. The tunic was white and gold, and the pattern of the brocade overlaid with gold braid and embroidery. The final nail in the financial coffin was the Queen Mother's costume for Act I, which was almost unbelievably lavish and said to cost £500. If a production was ever going to emerge from the chaos, then at least it was going to look beautiful if nothing else.

Much of the original music was put back, including the 'Pas des Fiancées' from the third act. This meant extra choreography for Orlikovsky. I was to dance the first night with Galina Samsova and was becoming increasingly worried about the time factor. Then to everyone's horror, Orlikovsky left, and about ten days before opening night, half the third act and none of the fourth act had been choreographed, so I went to Julian and pointed out that we had incredible problems to face. The Rank Organisation was also growing anxious. Their manager at the New Victoria, Stanley Fishman, came to me after Orlikovsky's departure to ask if I would finish off the production. I called in Joyce Graeme and between us we finished off the fourth act.

The strain was tremendous, having to get the production on as well as dancing in the opening performance. The company had not done this full length version before, so it was very important, but it literally bankrupted Festival Ballet. It was a production kept in the repertoire for a long time, although it was impossible to tour because it was so elaborate and cumbersome to move around from place to place. Beautiful though it looked, it was not enough to carry the company, and what was to have been a six-week season at the New Victoria ended after four weeks. *Swan Lake* had cost a total of £40,000 – exactly twice the budget which had been set for it. Arts Council chairman Lord Goodman came to the rescue, and there was an injection of funds to keep the company going.

Julian Braunsweg was replaced by Donald Albery as the company's Administrative Director, and I was appointed Artistic Director, with John Auld as my assistant. As I was also still principal dancer I found it impossible to continue doing two jobs at the same time. Not only was I constantly dancing, but I was also trying to direct. Eventually I had to tell Donald Albery that he must make a decision about what he wished me to do. I could either remain Artistic Director and give up as principal dancer, or continue to dance and relinquish my post as Artistic Director, which was the option I preferred. I was still young enough to go on dancing major roles and wanted to continue as long as I could. In the end I remained as principal dancer and gave up directing. Beryl Grey took over as Artistic Director in 1968.

Ruth Page was a great pioneer of dance in the United States, and I had met her in Chicago in 1947 when we stopped off there on our way to Australia with Rambert. She is one of the legendary figures of American dance, now in her eighties, and I am a great admirer of her energy and tenacity.

In 1966 she was Director of the Chicago Ballet, and invited me as a guest to dance *Nutcracker* at the Christmas season in Chicago. Afterwards the company always did a tour of six weeks – one year it was the West Coast, the second the East Coast, the third year the Mid West. It so happened I came in the tour of the Mid West – not the most glamorous part of the United States. I was dancing the pas de deux from Bournonville's *Flower Festival at Genzano*, and Act II of *Nutcracker*.

The tour took us thousands of miles, and to this day I cannot remember some of the towns we visited. We were driving between four and five hundred miles a day by bus, and for a dancer, having to sit still all day is no joke. We couldn't move or stretch, and had to drag ourselves from the bus, do barre, perform, return to the hotel (sometimes hideously uncomfortable), get up at 7 a.m. and set off again for the next place. It was sheer hell, and after six weeks I vowed I would never do such a thing again. Night after night dancing the same bread-and-butter ballets. God, I grew so sick of them. I dare not think of the number of times I have danced *Nutcracker* on all manner of stages – some agonisingly hard, and others dangerously slippery.

In New Orleans Ruth invited me to lunch at Antoine's, one of the city's smartest restaurants. One had to be correctly dressed to gain admittance – no man was allowed in without a tie, and the strictest formality was observed. Ruth and her husband arrived, Ruth turning up in a very chic Paris-made trouser suit.

'I'm sorry, Ma'am,' she was told. 'You cannot go into the restaurant in trousers.'

Ruth, being the person she is, did not turn a hair.

'Don't worry,' she replied. 'Hold on a moment.'

She disappeared into the ladies' room and removed the trousers. Her suit jacket came down just below her hips, and it looked as though she was wearing a brief mini-skirt, but she got away with it and we managed to have lunch!

I have always thought, even as a youngster, that whatever one achieved in life, or whatever gifts had been endowed, had to be paid for in some way. One must always pay back, and I had been blessed from the day I was born with the facility to dance. It was the law of nature, Karma, or whatever one cares to call it, that I had to pay for this gift, and my repayments began during the 1960s, lasting until comparatively recently. There was a terrific build-up of pressures from all directions – from home, from my work, financial worries, and anxiety about my health. Looking back, I realise it was something I had to go through, but at the time I thought, 'Why me? What have I done to deserve it?' We all assume we don't deserve the slings and arrows, but what is important is how we deal with them and what we learn from them.

For most of the sixties I was on tour in this country or abroad. It seemed I was never at home, which made for discontentment. I was aware of my own restlessness, and for the first time was beginning to sense there may come a time when I would fail. My ideals had always been so high; I was conceited enough never to believe in failure. Yet I had to accept that I had failed in holding my marriage together, my finances were in a mess, I knew I was beginning to drink too much, and there were times when my legs ached, which terrified me when I dwelt upon it. So I did not dwell upon it. I poured another drink and tried to forget it. The pains in my legs began in 1967, and earlier, and I put them to the back of my mind. I always hated fuss, and refused to acknowledge that instead of going away, the pain was getting worse.

I thought it was because I worked very hard and was always performing, but it was beginning to affect me mentally. Liz, my dresser, used to massage my legs to try and bring back the circulation, worriedly trying to persuade me to see a doctor, but I procrastinated. Deep down, I suppose I knew there was something badly wrong, but by refusing to do anything about it I would not have to acknowledge the unthinkable. It was probably just cramp anyway.

One evening I had been out to dinner with a doctor friend, Raymond Dixon-Firth, who lived in Curzon Street. We were returning to his place, and as we were walking along the road I had to stop for a while. It was nothing new; I was always having to stop if I walked any distance. Raymond turned round and asked what was the matter.

'It's my legs,' I replied. 'They've been hurting quite a bit lately. It's all right if I stop for a minute or two, but of course I can't stop on stage.' We paused for a time then I said, 'I'm OK now. Let's walk on.'

I had no idea at that time just how concerned Raymond had been by that small snippet of information. He did seem very anxious that I should go and see a specialist with him, and within a few days we had a consultation with one called Walter Somerville. I had all manner of tests done, and left his consulting rooms with some tablets, and strict instructions to stop smoking. It all seemed reasonable, and I was glad I had been to see somebody about the situation, and that something was being done. Life went on, so did I, and so did my dancing. I still had pains, but I continued to cope with them.

Donald Albery had invited Margot Fonteyn to join us as guest artist in Venice in February 1968. She was to dance *Sleeping Beauty* and *Night Shadow*. I had always loved *Night Shadow*, a beautiful Balanchine ballet which was mounted for us by John Taras. I had been in it with de Cuevas, dancing one of the Blackamoors in the ballroom scene. Now I was to dance one of my favourite roles – The Poet – with Fonteyn. I had first seen the role danced by George Skibine, a beautiful lyrical dancer and very fine actor who sadly died in 1981.

Fonteyn had never danced the role of The Sleepwalker, originally created by Danilova. She was about to leave for Finland with the second company of the Royal Ballet and we literally had one day in which to rehearse the ballet in November 1967, working in the Royal Ballet studios at Hammersmith. Margot learned the part in a matter of hours, and we did not see her again until February, in Venice, where she joined us after dancing at La Scala, Milan. It is an example of Fonteyn's wonderful artistry that not only had she learned *Night Shadow* in a very short time, but after not having met and rehearsed it for over two months, she remembered the whole thing. After the briefest rehearsal on the morning of our Venice performance she danced it to perfection.

I danced *Sleeping Beauty* in Venice with Dagmar Kessler, who was a lovely dancer. In 1977 she was the ballerina in Pittsburgh, which was ironic, because that was one of the less happy periods of my life. Galina Samsova and I were asked to dance in one of the operas being mounted during the Venice season – *Moses in Egypt*. It was a very modern set, and we had to dance a pas de deux on top of an enormous temple about thirty feet above the stage, which was terrifying, but we got through.

My drinking, which was becoming something of a problem, led me to be a guest of The Law for a night during the summer of 1968.

I had been to a Saturday night party near Reading during our Festival Hall season, and on the way home I managed to get a lift as far as Camberley, where I was dropped at the station. It had been a good party, and I had drunk more than I should have done, but that was nothing new. It was taking more and more drink to kill not only the ache in my legs, but my fear of what was happening. As I reached Camberley station in my befuddled state it did not cross my mind that it was 2 a.m. on a Sunday morning, and there was no London train until about 7 a.m. I found a telephone box, thinking I would try to call a taxi, but unfortunately the phone box had been vandalised. The receiver was broken, and when I discovered it was impossible to make a call I was so furious that I began to thump the coin box in sheer frustration. I was going to be stranded for hours in that God-forsaken place, probably sitting in some dismal waiting room, and I had to vent my wrath on something. My fist smashed down ferociously on the coin box.

The door of the telephone box was suddenly pulled open and I found myself face-to-face with a large policeman who had obviously witnessed the whole thing. It was like a scene from a comedy film. It had been my misfortune to choose a telephone box just by the police station – the perfect place! I had no doubt that the policeman believed I had also been responsible for the demolition of the receiver. It seemed there was to be no end to my night's adventures. The conscientious policeman decided to drag me off to the police station. I was still furious – now even more so, and was making a lot of noise, which did not help my case, so I was put into a cell to cool off and sober up.

They asked my name, and when they had all the requisite information they phoned my wife, and next morning put me on the London train. I received a summons for being drunk and disorderly, but the Press got hold of the story which appeared under a headline: DANCER IN CUSTODY FOR ATTEMPTED PHONE BOX THEFT. I certainly was not attempting to steal money from the phone box, and had no reason to do so. I had simply found a non-operational phone box when I was both drunk and in desperate need of a telephone, as a result of which I had lost my temper.

The night after the story appeared in the papers I was dancing at Festival Hall, and it was with considerable trepidation that I turned up that evening to face not only the audience, but my colleagues in the company. It was a packed house, and I was dancing *Etudes*, but I need not have worried – the audience loved it just the same!

On stage, clothed in the glamour of the role he is portraying, constantly striving for perfection, living in a carefully contrived stage world of beauty and great music, the dancer almost loses his own identity. The applause, the adulation is all part of the fairy story, but the real reward for me had always been the dancing itself. I had always known what I wanted to do, and was lucky that life had presented no obstacles which prevented me from using the talent I had. I enjoyed every aspect of my dancing life – the camaraderie of so many good friends in the company, the opportunity to travel, see fascinating places, meet interesting people, and above all, to dance, dance, dance. I never thought about it ending. Why should I? I was still a young man at the peak of my profession. Secure as I was in my happy, protected world, I didn't know that my luck had come to an end. My dancing time was running out.

At the end of the winter tour there came a nightmare day in Oxford when the pain was so intense and all-consuming that I shall never know how I got through the performance. It seared through me every time I moved, but having started the show I knew I had got to finish it, which – somehow – I managed to do. When I reached home in London my whole foot was icy cold and white. The doctor came, and had me whisked immediately into London Hospital for an infinitely delicate, complicated operation lasting seven hours.

While I was blissfully unconscious people kept phoning the hospital at what they imagined were decent intervals, only to be told that I was still in the operating theatre. I had apparently developed a massive blood clot in the main artery of my right leg, behind the knee, and it was touch and go whether or not I lost the lower half of my leg, because the clot was just on the point of breaking. It was only saved by hours of brilliant work by my surgeon, Douglas Eadie, who inserted a plastic by-pass. The blood condition which had killed my father was now evident in me.

It was only later I realised why Raymond, my doctor friend, had been so concerned when he heard how I had to stop and start when I was walking. This was a condition indicative of 'intermittent claudication', and a sign that something was seriously wrong with the circulation in my legs. With his experience he knew exactly what the

Production for Coventry Cathedral Re-building Fund. The 'Song of David' solo from Keith Lester's ballet *David, July, 1958*.

As Prince Florimund in *The Sleeping Beauty,* Royal Ballet, Covent Garden 1961.

Being presented to HRH Princess Margaret and HRH Princess Anne at a Gala Performance at the Royal Festival Hall in November, 1958.

In my dressing room at the New York State Theatre Lincoln Centre after performance of *Giselle* with Anton Dolin, Lucia Chase, the legendary Olga Spessivsteva and Ruth Ann Koesun, 1965. (*Photo by Jack Mitchell*).

(*Left*) With Anita Landa in *Witch Boy*, 1957 (*Photo by Roy Round*). (*Right*) Festival Ballet production of *The Sleeping Beauty,* 1967.

With Anita Landa, Anton Dolin, and the Festival Ballet company in *Witch Boy,* 1957.

signs meant, but how did one tell an internationally known male dancer, particularly a close friend, that the danger signs might mean the end of a career? I had also been kept unaware of the conversation Raymond had with Walter Somerville while I was dressing after the consultation with him. Mr Somerville had known then that my arteries were already beginning to close up. They had not wanted to alarm me, but they also knew that there was little they could do, apart from medication and good advice, to prevent the progress of the condition, and keep me going.

I was in hospital for three weeks, which seemed endless because I am very bad at doing nothing. Because my heart was strong I recovered well from the operation, and three months later, in June 1969, I was back on stage with Festival Ballet, making my return appearance in *Sleeping Beauty*. Everyone, including myself, marvelled at the rapidity of my recuperation. It seemed that all was well, and I was back to normal. But it was not as simple as it appeared. Physically I was in good shape, but from then on the the psychological repercussions began to take effect. I knew, deep down, that I was weakened by the experience, and that my dancing was wholly dependent upon the lifespan of a piece of plastic in my leg. I tried not to think about it – after all, people had heart pace-makers and plastic hip joints and still went on living, I told myself. But then came a small voice which said, 'Yes, but they don't live by dancing.'

Then I would feel a sense of shock, and naturally begin to have misgivings about what I was doing. My legs were my lifeline – the only means of retaining my position at the top of my profession. Dancing had always been my life ever since I was a small boy; I had always taken it for granted. Never had the nightmare thought crossed my mind that my legs would give out. I realised, of course, that one day I would have to stop dancing, but not for years . . . not until I was too old. A premature retirement was something which had never entered my head, but now the unconsidered and unthinkable was becoming a possible reality I found myself under ever increasing stress. I was still young, I was at the top, and somehow I had to keep going!

Beryl Grey was Artistic Director of the company when I returned. At the end of that London season, just before we were about to leave for Spain, I went in one morning to find a state of total confusion.

There was a great deal of anger among the dancers, who were threatening to go on strike because, they alleged, Beryl Grey had sacked nine dancers, including three or four soloists. As senior member of the company I was asked if I would represent them, and go with them to put their case to Equity, although the row had nothing to do with me.

Unfortunately the newspapers got hold of the story and the facts became somewhat blurred and distorted, making it appear that I was trying to usurp Beryl Grey and take over her job. This was a ridiculous suggestion, as I had already held the post of Artistic Director three years previously, and had resigned, so it must have been obvious that I had no wish to take over the company again. Nevertheless, the publicity had undoubtedly succeeded in branding me as the ringleader of the revolt. As a result I was called to the office by the Administrator Wilfred Stiff, on the last night of the season, just twenty-four hours before the company was due to leave for Spain, and was told that I would not be needed on the Spanish tour.

I could hardly believe my ears. The misunderstanding had obviously reached mammoth proportions. By way of compensation for the ban, I was told not to worry, as my salary would still be paid even though my services were not required. That was all very well, but I was angry, sad, and very upset that something like that could happen, especially as the situation had arisen purely through a misrepresentation of the facts. My first reaction was to argue and fight back, but then I decided that whatever I said at that stage would simply make matters worse, so I decided to swallow the unpleasant medicine and keep my mouth shut about the whole thing. The company certainly did not need any more publicity on the issue, and neither did I.

So Festival Ballet left for Spain without me. I had first toured Spain in 1949 and was perhaps the best known English male dancer on the Continent. At the time of this dispute my name was always on Festival Ballet contracts, together with Samsova, Prokovsky, and other leading dancers, stipulating our appearances. The result was that on the Spanish tour these requirements were not met, and the impresarios responsible for the arrangements were not pleased. The tour was not an outstanding success, and the company duly returned to London.

Still no approach had been made to me to dance in the forthcoming season at the Royal Festival Hall, although I was still on full salary. I hated my enforced inactivity and the reason for it. The company was to embark in September for the first tour of Japan, and out of the blue I had a call from the British Council, under whose auspices the trip was to be made. I was both surprised and delighted to hear that the British Council had informed the company that unless I was on the tour, it would be cancelled. I was therefore reinstated and asked to go to Japan. It meant a lot of red faces all round, but there was no point in gloating. I felt justice had been done, and I am not one to bear a grudge. I was re-admitted to the fold and was overjoyed to be back.

The world of the theatre is noted for gossip and backstage sniping, and throughout my career I have often been surprised to discover jealousies in people I was hardly aware of, although I can honestly say I have neither been jealous nor envious of another dancer. I never felt I had any reason to be, and therefore could never understand why there were those who indulged in back-biting against me, except that such human frailties are usually the result of fear of one kind or another – fear of failure, of losing one's job, or even one's identity.

But accepting these reasons did not make it less upsetting during the bad times to discover two-facedness, often in people I had helped. There were times when I cursed myself for my naivety, for trusting everyone. It takes some kind of saint to make allowances all the time, and none of us are saints. Fortunately there is always some kind of protection which for a time provides a cocoon of oblivion. We are unaware of the stabs in the back until afterwards; at the time we cannot believe in such betrayal. Certainly if I had been aware of everything going on behind my back at the time it was actually happening I would have been a neurotic heap. Had I known what I was supposed to have done or not done I could have become suicidal, so I closed my eyes to it all and tried to get on with what I was there to do, which was to dance.

For another year after my operation I danced on, under enormous pressure, putting myself on the rack, often in pain, pushing myself to the limits to fulfil expectations of me, to maintain my reputation, and to satisfy myself. It is always said that once one has reached the top, the only direction open to one is downwards. Perfection is a hard taskmaster, and I had never aimed at anything less, so I battled on to stay where I was – at the top.

How stupid of me to try and cheat Fate, because it simply dealt me another horrifying blow. A second clot developed in the thigh of my left leg, necessitating another operation. Again I recovered and clambered back to health, returning to the stage at a Gala Performance at the London Coliseum on 22nd June 1971, when I danced my variation from *Variations for Four*. I was terribly nervous, but it was wonderful to be back, and both Press and public gave me a heart-warming reception.

As one paper kindly put it: 'The Gala was highlighted by the return of John Gilpin, making a rare and rapturously received appearance after recovering from his thrombosis.'

Superficially, yes, it could be said that I had recovered, and I could even dance again, but it was an incredibly difficult period for me, and I could not always meet all my commitments to dance. Stories began to circulate within the ballet world about my non-appearances at performances at which I was billed to dance. Charity does not always abound when people wish to gossip, and I did not want charity, but truth did not always take precedence either. The real reason was a deep-rooted fear – a terror of not knowing how I would be when I got on stage, or what damage I was doing every time I danced. It was also very painful, and there were times when I literally had to force myself on to the stage. Each performance was like tackling a marathon. Was I going to last out? What would happen if . . . ?

I found that adverse weather conditions began to affect my legs, which became like personalised barometers. On one occasion in Paris the weather was freezing cold and my legs felt like lead. I was due to dance *Witch Boy* and I suddenly realised perfectly well that the task was totally beyond me.

'I'm sorry,' I had to announce defeatedly, 'I just cannot do it.'

The knowledge that I now had not one weakened leg, but two, made it even harder to perform. The inner tension was tremendous, not knowing what was going to happen to my legs on stage. I did not want to talk about it, so said nothing, but it was very difficult to keep up any semblance of a façade.

I found I was beginning to be absolutely petrified before going on stage – something I had never experienced in my life. I had always been very excited, and even slightly nervous before going on, but the instant I got on stage it disappeared. Now I had a gnawing, physical nausea in which I would suffer agonising days and sleepless nights before a performance. It was very hard to make people understand. Why should they? They only saw the leaping, spinning automaton, taking curtain calls with a bright smile. I was the only one who knew I was in pain, and very frightened. There was also the question of pride, as I hated letting people down, and did not want to let myself down by turning in a bad performance. Lynn Seymour has described a ballet performance as a bullfight, and certainly at that time I felt that each appearance was like facing death in an arena.

Conflicts were coming at me from all directions, in my personal life as well as my career. Although my marriage had been finished, in effect, for years, and Sally and I had not been living together for some time, I still had financial responsibilities and emotional ties with my daughter. When I divorced Sally in 1970 it was all quite amicable, but it was still an upheaval. I was glad to have things cleared up for Tracy's sake, because her security must have been disturbed by our separation. The only time I felt emotionally free was when I was dancing. Apart from that I kept things hidden away and suppressed, so that the tensions inevitably built up. I did not find it easy to talk about myself, let alone about my personal affairs and what I knew to be my sheer physical weaknesses. As a principal dancer one never mentioned such things, but the operations have been public knowledge, and I knew that other people knew what had happened. It did not make life any easier, and only served to make dancing more difficult.

The important thing about adversity is what we learn from it. I was a slow learner, but gradually, after each operation I got through, and each obstacle I overcame, I found myself becoming aware of things of which I was previously in ignorance – myself as a human being, my place in society, and where I stood as an individual stripped of the trappings of fame. After years of being spoiled and pampered within the protection of a large company I was suddenly out of my environment, and life had changed drastically. Never, until I left Festival Ballet had I needed to do the ordinary things of life, even to making travel arrangements or booking hotels. It had always been done for us. I was alone when I stopped dancing – no longer John Gilpin the dancer, but John Gilpin the person, and I was totally unprepared for the revelation which had been so prematurely forced upon me. It was like going back to childhood, to an early age even before a professional dancing career was envisaged for me, and that was a long way back. I had been the brilliant prodigy, and the more I achieved, the more was expected of me. It had never been a struggle to fulfil such expectations in the early days. Yes, I worked hard, but I enjoyed it, and was simply polishing a natural gift with which I was born, and for which I have always been grateful. Now I was learning what life might have been like without that gift; the human body was vulnerable, and mine was no different from anybody else's, despite its finely tuned abilities.

During the last seven years I have been pulled back to look at myself and my life. The great thing at the back of my mind was to survive, which I did. I still want to attain certain ideals, and although I am not naturally a pessimist I have learned caution. This does not mean I allow myself to be hampered by doubts, and I still go ahead if it seems the right thing to do.

The ballet is a small, insular world. Within the protective shell of the big company one's whole life becomes a round of just class, rehearsal, performance. Everything is already there; one does not have time to think, and there is little space for concern about one's private life. I don't like the word 'dedicated', but dancing is a complete dedication, and it is difficult for dancers when they ultimately retire if they have no alternative talent or qualification to fill the void. My commitments will always be involved with the theatre, but in addition to what I would wish to achieve for myself, I now believe I can give to the younger generation – things I have absorbed from very great people. One has a duty to give, and I have had such tremendous experience that I must pass it on.

As well as giving on the professional side I feel I can now give on a purely human basis because I have become more tolerant of the ordinary abrasions of life. It is a salutory lesson to know oneself – if one ever does – and upon reflection I know where I went wrong, and what my failings are. I now know that I was not ready for marriage in 1960, even at the age of thirty. Maybe I will never be ready for that kind of commitment because I regard myself as self-reliant and self-sufficient, which perhaps in itself is a form of conceit. I love having interesting people around me, but I don't mind being alone – as long as it is not for ever. To some extent I will always want people and excitement. Freedom is at the root of my character, and to be tied down is like a prison sentence. This is one aspect of me which never changes.

In 1971 it seemed that everything had come to an end. My marriage was dead and gone long ago, I had financial problems, and my career as a dancer was drawing to a close after all the years of pushing myself to the limits in order to maintain it.

I had always enjoyed parties, company, and social drinking. Now I was not so anxious to meet people, and as the early seventies went on so my social drinking gave way to private drinking. I did not want to know about the ballet because I was no longer part of it, as I thought. I was a nobody. Self-pity set in, and a great deal of bitterness. I found I was pouring myself a drink to drown the physical and mental pain, and because I chose to spend a lot of time by myself I was pouring more and more drinks, almost unthinkingly. It was the start of a downward spiral into my own personal hell, and somehow I didn't even care.

Chapter Eleven

It was 1974, and I had come out of hospital after the third operation. Dolin had taken a house in Capri, and he thought it would be good for me to get away from England for a time, so I agreed to go.

When we arrived in Capri it was winter, and freezing cold – a far cry from those hot sunny days I had spent there years previously when I had been a healthy young dancer with legs giving no hint of troubles to come. I installed myself at the villa, which was taken for a year, and I spent about four months on the island. A good friend was living there – Marjorie Ellis, whom I had met in the early seventies, and she was a great help, although I had started to drink quite a lot. I was still having a great deal of trouble with my legs, which were constantly painful. Marjorie thought that exercise would help to keep my mind off things, so simply to avoid upsetting her I would agree to go on long hikes with her, even though at times I was in absolute agony.

The pain led to my having a few more drinks to drown it, and there was no stopping me, so the whole cycle of events insiduously began to build up.

I came back to London, and then had to go to New York for Ballet Theatre's 35th Anniversary Gala. I spent three weeks in New York, and was congratulating myself that I had not been drunk for some time, but something triggered it off again. I became ill and had to return to London, but once I had recovered it was essential that I had something to occupy myself. I was asked if I would do some teaching for Errol Addison at the Dance Centre while he was away for two months.

It seemed like a good idea, and would at least give me something to do, so I took it on. I soon realised it was not the answer to any of the problems besetting me at that time. It proved to be a thoroughly frustrating exercise, and having to be at the studios each morning at

11.30 to cope with about forty or fifty people was impossible. If I had been perfectly healthy it would have been a different matter, but in the state I was, I could not tussle with it so I gave it up.

A kind of haze descended, mostly alcohol induced. Life was often a series of blanks because I simply did not remember what I had done. At night-time I used to dread going to bed because of the apprehension of waking up shaking. I had to drink first thing in the morning to stop the shakes, reaching for the vodka before I could start the day. It became a nightmare of running away – fleeing from myself and from all responsibilities. I shut myself away because I thought I looked awful, even though people said I didn't, and I reached the stage when I would only go out after dark. I was petrified of the telephone and would not answer it, nor would I open letters. Everything was slipping out of control and there was nothing I could do about it. The point came when I did not know what I was doing, and was in the depths of despair.

I blacked out, had the shakes, and became desperate if there wasn't a bottle in the house. It became a life of waiting for the pubs or off-licences to open. I was calculating enough to go to different places, devising a rota system so that I would not be recognised in the same place too often. Drinking never made me happy. People think it will produce a kind of spurious happiness, that they will lose inhibition and become the life and soul of the party. But in the end, everything in excess only brings the direst misery. The life I led in the public eye made it more difficult for me, but that was part and parcel of the price I had to pay for what I was and who I had become.

From what I gather, I was not a very good drunk, if there is such a thing. I could become very violent sometimes, but on occasions I would be excessively jolly and like a naughty child, which must have been very boring for everyone. I was usually at my worst when I was at home and shut away. I would pace up and down the long corridor in the apartment, going out of my mind. One does terrible things and knows nothing about them until being told afterwards. People come to you afterwards and relate what you have done. 'My God,' you reflect in horror. 'Did I really do that?'

Sometimes I would find myself in places and not have the first idea how I had got there. I would stare around blankly and ask myself, 'What am I doing here?' which I found terrifying.

All this drama and futility went on until Christmas of 1975, and Marjorie had come from Capri to spend it with us. It was absolutely catastrophic, what little I can remember of it, and by the time January came my doctor and surgeon were very concerned about me. I think if I had gone on drinking for another month I would have been dead, and I was aware, even through the alcoholic fog of the previous weeks, that they had been trying to get me to go for treatment. They kept talking about a place called St Bernard's, and though I did not know what or where it was, I knew in my mind that it meant something quite drastic.

Just after my birthday in February 1976 there came the morning when I knew people were coming to take me to St Bernard's. Patrick was at home, in the apartment, my doctor came, and my surgeon arrived. Because I knew this was coming up I had been drinking all night, so was in no mood to see reason. After all, I thought, they could not force me to go.

I faced them defiantlyas they all tried to be placatory. They were not going to organise my life and make me do what I did not wish to do.

'I'm not going!' I shouted at them, and promptly locked myself in my bedroom where nobody was able to get at me. There I sat, belligerent, desperately miserable, and hopelessly, helplessly drunk, while on the other side of the door everyone was wondering what the next move was going to be and how they were going to cope with the impasse. As I sat there, even though my brain was so sodden with alcohol, I became aware of some message being relayed deep in the recesses of my befuddled mind. It came quite suddenly.

'Well,' a voice seemed to say, 'do you want to live or do you want to die? If you want to die, go out there and tell them all to get the hell out of it because you're not going . . . Or do you want to survive?'

Suddenly there came an awareness of what I must do. God knows where it came from. I sat there a little longer before crawling to my feet. I crossed the room, unlocked the door and opened it.

I stood there unsteadily, glaring at the anxiously waiting group. 'All right,' I announced. 'I'll go.'

A car arrived, and I dimly remember getting into it. After that there was nothing. There came a period of total blackness into which I sank almost gratefully.

There was no recollection of anything else until I woke up facing a wall – a strange wall, and everything seemed grey. I hazily came to, raised my head and looked around. I saw I was in a long sort of ward with lots of beds and strange people, and I had a terrifying moment of panic.

I had no idea where I was or how I had got there. Both questions were eventually answered – I was in St Bernard's Hospital in Southall, Middlesex, and I had been there for two days.

There came a period of adjustment, of getting to grips with the fact that I was there because I was an alcoholic, confined to hospital to be dried out. It was horrifying, and at times unbelievable, but I knew that if I wanted to be cured I was going to have to stick with it to the bitter end. There was no going back. If I did so I would simply condemn myself to a drunken death. Impossible! Not me – not the great dancer, the fairy-tale prince. This couldn't be me, and this was not happening to me . . . . But it was, it was.

Patients came from all walks of life. There were doctors, writers, a veterinary surgeon . . . the grip of alcohol is not discriminating, and I was no different from anybody else. I found it disturbing that drug addicts were treated in the same ward as alcoholics, but this was from sheer necessity as there were not enough hospital beds to treat them separately, which is a sad picture of today's so-called civilised society. It was pathetic to hear the young people telling how it had all started. Usually the beginnings of their downfall lay in their environment and upbringing. Many had left school early, or had simply dropped out and started on drugs just for the hell of it. No matter how harmless or mild some drugs are said to be, it was quite clear that there is no such thing as a harmless drug. One gets used to a sensation until the tolerance wears off, and it becomes necessary to move on to something stronger. More potent drugs . . . more bottles of drink . . . the picture is the same.

I found myself under tremendous tension the whole time I was undergoing treatment, but the doctors were wonderfully understanding.

Not that I was in receipt of any special privileges; there was no reason why I should be, and I was treated exactly the same as everyone else. Those in charge were amazed that, coming from my glamorous background (as they thought) of theatre and ballet, I weathered the tough atmosphere so well. It was a searing, opening experience, and was by no means easy, but I was quite determined to stick it out for the recommended three months, and I did so.

The drying-out process was petrifying. There was a period of craving and withdrawal symptoms during which one experienced shakes and sweats, hallucinations and nightmares, with no proffered relief by the administration of drugs. All we had were vitamin injections and those given as a deterrent because mixed with alcohol they made the patient violently ill. In private clinics the initial withdrawal symptoms are helped by sedation. In St Bernard's it was the policy not to make it too easy, and perhaps rightly so. One had to bear with it and come through. I saw one or two youngsters go overboard during that period, and they were put in isolation for twenty-four hours. The first three or four weeks were absolute hell, the discipline tough and relentless. For three weeks one was not even allowed out to the hospital shop in the grounds. Visitors were not allowed for a month. There was another patient there from the theatre, who was there when I arrived. He took me under his wing and was my lifeline during those first weeks. He was older than I, and became a very good friend.

There was nothing to stop me from walking out after the minimum stay of twenty-eight days. Many patients thought they were then cured, but during my three months I saw them return time after time. The desire to be cured was not strong enough to overcome the need to pour that first drink.

I was determined to kick that need because I knew that until I had done so, what was left of my life would be sickness, misery, and total futility. With this in mind I put up with the often abhorrent tasks imposed by hospital discipline, which were completely foreign to me after what had been, I suppose, a charmed existence. From dancing legendary heroes in theatres throughout the world, from the limelight and public adulation, mixing with royalty and the great names of the theatre, I found myself washing floors, cleaning out lavatories, and dragging heavy food trolleys across the grounds. The washing-up for about a hundred people was what I loathed above all else – plunging my hands into that great vat of greasy water turned my stomach.

After five weeks I graduated to the status of Group Leader, which meant I had to assign my group members to their weekly tasks, making a rota. It also meant I had a responsibility towards new patients. One of the most distressing experiences was on a Monday when new patients arrived, often fighting drunk, and one had to help with them. Some arrived with relatives and sat outside drinking from bottles before they were made to come in.

It was part of the therapy that there was little free time. There was a constant mobility of one kind or another, and a continual round of lectures, discussions and group therapy. Visitors were not allowed during the early weeks, but later in the course of treatment patients' families were invited to lectures so they could assist with rehabilitation after discharge. I found it hard to come to terms with never being alone for any length of time. After four weeks I was delighted to be moved to a single room. Even then there was no respite from the perpetual motion, and nobody was allowed to lie around on a bed during the day.

Bedtime was at 9.30, and a group leader had to be up at 6 a.m. and see that everybody else was up by seven o'clock. Throughout all those weeks I found it almost impossible to sleep. I seldom slept more than a couple of hours during any night, so it was bliss to be allowed home for my first weekend. If ever there was a test of willpower it was at the end of the weekends at home, having gone back to the comfort of the flat and knowing one had to leave it on a Sunday evening to go back into the rigorous spartan atmosphere of the hospital. There was always such a great urge not to return. Perhaps I was cured; maybe I could now control things for myself without the imposed discipline from outside. Did I really need to go back? Nobody could force me to do so, and I was well aware that I could have walked out of the whole scene at any time. But somehow I always went back, to face the inevitable tests the moment I arrived on the hospital premises, to see if I had drunk anything during the weekend. On one occasion I had taken a sleeping pill in order to get a good night's rest, with the result that the barbiturate showed up in my test and I lost the privilege of having the next weekend at home.

I suggested that I might give movement and gym sessions, an idea that met with approval, and to my surprise these diversions were very well attended. Most of the inmates had been quite unused to such activity, but it was amazing how many attended and thoroughly enjoyed the new experience.

'When you leave St Bernard's, are you going to drink or are you going to be a teetotaller?' It was an unavoidable question, and one which was often asked during our stay there. There were the few who knew, deep down, that they would never be able to make an honest undertaking of that kind, so they said they would only have the odd social drink. After several weeks inside, having seen patients go home and return defeated, I was quite convinced that there was only one answer. What you learn from being an alcoholic, and what you hope to apply is that you will never drink again – ever. It takes about six months to get the alcohol out of the system, but one slip can set back the whole process of drying out.

I had been discharged for six months when I had a slip. At first I had been wary all the time.

'My God,' I thought. 'All around me – everywhere I move – everyone drinks. How am I going to be able to resist?'

I moved in a circle where people drank freely and I was the odd one out. It seemed incredible, but even after all I had been through I was reluctant to believe that I could not control my intake of drink. I make the excuse that I drank that one glass of white wine because I was lonely, having been left alone in the apartment for a weekend.

'Just one drink,' I thought. 'Let's see what happens.'

I was sure I could stop after that, and was convinced of my own ability to apply the brake. I should have believed what had been drummed into us during those miserable weeks in hospital, but somehow one is always sure that weakness is in other people and never in oneself. It isn't true. Within a week I was in a private clinic, where I stayed for a fortnight. I now know without a shadow of doubt that if I started to drink again I should be a raving alcoholic in no time at all.

Self-analysis is one of the disciplines imposed during a stay in an alcoholic unit, and one of the revealing aspects of the system was a regular session called 'Life Stories', in which we had to write down and read to other patients the whole of our life history. When it was time for me to read my story I was absolutely petrified. At the same time as trying to execute this piece of 'homework' we were also going through the psychological hell of drying out. By the time the day came for my reading I had not even managed to finish writing it. The morning I was due to deliver my life story to the assembled patients, I had worked myself up into a state of nerves far worse than I had ever experienced on any first night in the theatre. Everyone knew who I was, of course, and I think they were curious about me; intrigued to know why I was there, doing things the hard way. They were therefore looking forward to hearing my story, and perhaps in some way waiting to knock it, which they were more than capable of doing. I had seen it happen to others.

The stories were read in groups of four – two men and two women. All the patients met together in the main building to listen, and at the end they all fired questions at the speakers, under the supervision of the medical team and groups running the wards. Just before I got up to read I had a strange thought from the past. It was a memory of Noël Coward, one of those glamorous characters from a totally different world from that in which I now found myself. The recollection of his past advice came through as though he were sitting there talking to me again.

'John, whenever you are speaking,' Noël had said sagely, 'remember to be loud, and slow, and clear.'

I said this to myself and started on my story, which lasted for three quarters of an hour and received tremendous applause! I knew they had believed me because they only questioned me for five minutes, whereas I had seen some speakers grilled for an hour because the others did not believe their stories. Many fantasised about their past, but having listened to so many I began to know myself when people were lying.

If one could learn from the disciplines of St Bernard's, which was not easy, then there was great benefit. It is perhaps one of the most successful places of its kind in the country. The tragedy is that they need to exist at all.

When I first came out I felt terribly small. When I went into a room full of people I felt like a midget looking at another world. Then slowly, after about two months, everything came back into perspective again, but it was as though I was an alien, even among my friends. I had to start proving myself all over again, as though beginning a new life – which I suppose I was. I had to regain the confidence of friends and associates, and at that time I learned a lot about who my real friends were. It was disconcerting to realise, as I did, that I could count them on the fingers of one hand.

What never ceases to amaze me is that people who know all I went through will still unthinkingly offer me a drink. It is often assumed that because I don't drink, I therefore automatically object to those who do.

'Do you mind if we drink?' I am sometimes asked nervously.

My reply is that I don't mind at all. I move in a section of society where there are constant parties and everyone drinks like a fish, but it no longer bothers me, and I would not dream of wrecking a party by seeming to be prissy. People look shocked when I say I am an alcoholic. It is a difficult thing to have to say, and fortunately I rarely have to say it, except when somebody is trying to force a drink upon me. People sometimes ask my advice about drinking, and I will give it, but in the end it is up to the person himself to effect the cure. Many doctors still do not realise what it really means to be an alcoholic.

In St Bernard's they were always using the phrase, 'When you get outside . . . ' and coming out was in a way like being released from prison. What I learned is that the old adage about 'anything in moderation' just is not true. You either drink or you don't drink, and if you happen to be an alcoholic then you go on until you kill yourself.

The last time I danced classically—*Variations for Four,* Tokyo, 1976.

In rehearsal for *Carmina Burana,* Madrid, 1978. Possibly my last dancing role?

Making-up for Oberon in Lindsay Kemp's production of *A Midsummer Night's Dream.* Parma, Italy, March 1981.

First production of *Invitation to the Dance* at Stephenville Festival, Newfoundland, July 1980. Myself (right), with Jeff Pitcher and Terri Snelgrove.

Chapter Twelve

I had been asked by Tokyo Ballet if I would go out there in October 1976. They wanted me to produce Dolin's *Variations for Four* and dance my original role in it. The invitation arrived in April.

'Why not?' I thought. 'I'll try.'

So I started back to class again, thinking I had all those months from April to October. I worked and worked, trying to get back into form. I had not danced for so long that it was a great struggle. I was no longer in my twenties, or even my thirties, which made it even harder. Dancing is like athletics, and one has to keep up the constant training. I knew I had years of experience behind me, which was a help, but it was not good enough to see me over this hurdle without a lot of additional work.

In June I spent a month in Capri, still trying to keep up some programme of training. Then I went on to Varna with Patrick, where we worked on *Etudes* with Patrick Dupond, and I started back to class. I was still unsure about whether I would be able to dance in Tokyo. *Variations for Four* is a purely virtuoso piece, and had therefore to be immaculate. There must be no question of cheating or muddling my way through, which would never have done for me anyway. I really had to get it absolutely right. I wrote to Tokyo saying I would be delighted to go and teach them the ballet, but I was not sure whether or not I would be able to dance in it until August, by which time I would know just how competent I was likely to be.

By the end of August Tokyo was growing impatient, and I was still working hard to try and get back some of my old capabilities. I had a telegram saying they must know immediately whether I was going to dance.

It was a big decision to make, but I thought I was in pretty good shape, even though my legs were quite painful. I could certainly dance, but only with a great deal of discomfort.

During August I gave a series of Master Classes at the Royal Academy of Dancing, and in September went to Paris to produce *Pas de Quatre*, from there going to Scotland to work with Scottish Ballet. Despite all my work – or maybe because of it – my legs were beginning to give trouble, and did not seem to have any strength. The muscles did not pull as they should. I still did classes in Scotland and rehearsed the company, continuing to attend London classes upon my return.

On 8th October I left for Tokyo, where I stayed six weeks, and managed to get through two performances of *Variations for Four*. It was a traumatic experience because I was extremely nervous, not knowing whether my legs were going to last out. It was just like the old days, after the first operations. Why did I have to put myself through this kind of anguish?

When it was all over I thought, 'Well, that's it. I have now got dancing out of my system.' I had tried to accomplish what I used to be able to do, and it was now for me to accept the facts calmly and logically, which was not easy. There comes a moment in any dancing career when one has to give up anyway, but I knew that if my legs had been normal I would have been able to go on dancing other roles which were less technically demanding. What was so difficult to acknowledge was that my legs were not normal, and it was a grim moment of truth when I realised I was unable to dance any longer.

After returning from Tokyo I went to Cuba for Alicia Alonso's National Ballet of Cuba Festival, and spent Christmas in New York. It was not a particularly happy time, and I vividly recall spending Christmas Eve entirely alone, watching television until midnight and feeling very sad and depressed.

I was approached to join Los Angeles Ballet as joint Artistic Director, but American dance critic Walter Terry also told me that Pittsburgh Ballet Theatre was looking for a Director, so while I was in America I went to see the company. It was quite a small one, and very young. After some discussions I was offered the post of Artistic Director, which I accepted. I felt it was time to branch out, but I was not sure in which direction. I hated the idea of not dancing. It was in my blood, and having spent a lifetime on the stage it is very difficult to stop performing. I did not want to settle down and open a school, which is always the most obvious solution to occur to an ex-dancer. At that stage in my life I was far too restless to start teaching day in, day out.

People still keep urging me to teach. 'Why don't you go and teach at the Royal Academy of Dancing?' they ask. The answer is that I cannot see myself either teaching or sitting on endless committees, which one inevitably has to do if accepting that way of life.

My arrival in Pittsburgh was accompanied by high hopes, but unfortunately they were not fulfilled. Having signed my contract I arrived to begin work with the company to discover that there were only twenty dancers available. This lack of numbers was in no way commensurate with the pre-arranged repertoire for the coming season, with which I had been presented along with my twenty dancers. As a package deal it was quite impossible. There was a full-length Prokofiev *Romeo and Juliet*, a full-length *Swan Lake*, and a full length *Nutcracker*, not to mention other short ballets. With such a programme to prepare, my first task had to be to recruit more dancers.

There was no school attached to the company, so there were no resources upon which to draw. To add to my difficulties I discovered that all the ballets had to be re-choreographed. The man who had founded the company had been a folk dancer in the Yugoslav army, and the first Artistic Director had choreographed all the classics from films of the Bolshoi Ballet, on which whole sequences had been based. Pittsburgh is one of the wealthiest cities in America, but unlimited money does not necessarily make a ballet company. There was a certain arrogance about their attitude, and they delighted in saying that Pittsburgh Ballet Theatre was the only company apart from American Ballet Theatre which toured the great classics, but I was far from satisfied with the standards they set.

It was March 1977 when I arrived, and the season was due to open in September, so time was short. The weeks went by, and I thought I would go out of my mind as I tried to find choreographers as well as auditioning dancers in New York who decided they did not want to work in Pittsburgh. Somehow I managed to get the ballets on, but it was not one of the most pleasant experiences of my life, and an undertaking I should not care to repeat. I found myself tied in so many directions. Apart from the job I was supposed to do as Artistic Director, I was also Administrator and general factotum. I was doing everyone's job and found the greatest difficulty in doing anything to my satisfaction, in addition to which I was only able to spend five or six hours a week with the company itself, which should have been the first priority. I had been Artistic Director with Festival Ballet, but that had been an entirely different experience. There I had a large company behind me and lots of additional assistance.

I soon felt very isolated in the vast city of Pittsburgh, and desperately miserable, with too much to do and no support troops to help smooth the way. My stay was only made bearable by the presence of an old friend, Patricia Stander, who had been with the Royal Ballet and Festival Ballet, and was in Pittsburgh just when I needed encouragement. It was a great cultural shock, coming from the European ballet background, and with the training I had received all my life, to observe the ease with which they thought ballets could be flung on to a stage. I resented the haphazard approach and casual attitude having experienced so many years of being forced to give meticulous attention to detail. As time went on I began to feel like a caged leopard, and after a year decided I could not go on. I was not able to do what I wished, nor was I giving the company what I would have liked to give. It suddenly became vital that I got away, so I tendered my resignation and left Pittsburgh, feeling very homesick and disillusioned. I had learned a lot from the whole experience, but once again it had been given to me the hard way.

It was wonderful to be back in England, and a tremendous relief to be away from the pressures of the previous year. I was delighted to see all my old friends again, and being back home had never before been so attractive and secure. I began to catch up with everyone again, and was invited with Patrick to Kathleen Gordon's annual birthday party, which was always a great gathering of ballet personalities – Margot Fonteyn was there, Ninette de Valois, dear Marie Rambert, and countless others, and it seemed we all never stopped talking.

I spotted a little man standing over in one corner. His face was familiar, and I was sure we had met, but I couldn't remember his name. I had a feeling he wanted to talk to me and sure enough, halfway through the party he crossed the room towards me.

'John, you look marvellously well,' he said. 'I know what you've been through, and I've never seen you looking so fit.'

That was nice, but I still did not know who he was, and did not have the courage to tell him. Had I really met him before? If so, I had no idea where the meeting was.

'As I was standing on the other side of the room,' he went on, 'I saw the most extraordinary gold aura around you. I can see you've been through a great deal. I know all about the legs, of course.'

I continued to smile pleasantly as I tried to rack my brains for some knowledge of who he was, when suddenly he said, 'Can I see your hands?'

Surprised at the strange request, I showed him my hands, which he began to study.

'It's going to take time,' he announced thoughtfully, 'and there will be a couple of setbacks, but I can tell you that the second half of your life is going to be even more successful than the first part.'

I'm not sure whether one believes this sort of thing or not, but strangely enough, all through my life various people have told me my later years would be the most important. This man said I would be very successful in everything I would do or re-do. It would all take time, but I mustn't worry.

I had not been back from Pittsburgh very long when there was a telephone call from Anna Lazarro, who ran Ballet Classico of Madrid. She wanted to speak to Patrick, but as she had been asking me to go and dance for her company for years, she took the opportunity of asking me if I would care to go Spain to do a TV series she was directing, in which Patrick was also taking part.

'What do you want me to do?' I asked cautiously.

'The show is in two parts,' she explained. 'I would like Dolin to talk in both parts, and would you come and dance?'

I told her it very much depended upon how much dancing she needed me to do. Apart from my leg problems I had not been in training while in Pittsburgh, but fortunately I had been attending the Royal Ballet School for class since my return, which was gradually dispelling the stiffness accumulated after a year of sitting at a desk. Anna asked if I could dance one of my variations from *Variations for Four*, which was a pretty tall order in my current condition. I replied that I would be delighted to go and talk, but when Dolin and I arrived in Spain I agreed to dance my Variation in the second half of the programme.

Anna was nothing if not persuasive. 'Could you not possibly do something in the first half as well?' she asked.

The programme was to be filmed, so I decided to risk things still further. I agreed to dance Flemming Flindt's *Variation* in the first half of the programme.

Everything went well during my performance of Flemming's *Variation*, but my own was much longer and more intensive. We surmounted the difficulty by filming it in two parts, one twenty minutes after the other, as my legs were not strong enough to sustain the longer solo. Anna was pleased with the result, and invited me to go back in May and dance as a guest with her company in Madrid. She told me she had a new ballet she had always had in mind for me if I ever danced with her company – *Carmina Burana*, not the Carl Orff version, but the one with thirteenth-century music.

Before I accepted that, I had another commitment in Canada, so I crossed the Atlantic again and helped Dolin remount *Giselle* for Les Grands Ballets Canadiens in Montreal, taught at the National, and coached. That completed, I went to Madrid to rehearse, and stayed there for six weeks. Anna had made the ballet quite hard; there was more acting than dancing, but there was still a lot of dancing to cope with. My legs were painful most of the time, but somehow I managed to do what was required of me.

Dolin in the meantime had been in Toronto, playing Herod in *Salome* for the Lindsay Kemp Company. While he was there he had met the actor and playwright Maxim Mazumdar, also in Toronto at that time with his one-man play *Oscar Remembered*, based on Oscar Wilde. Having seen the play, Dolin was greatly impressed by his talent, and asked Maxim if he would consider writing a one-man play for him. Maxim did so, and the result was *Conversations* which he has now played many times.

Maxim came to London for two Sunday performances of *Oscar Remembered* at the Mayfair Theatre, which of course I was unable to see. He wrote to me in Madrid, saying he would like to come and see me dance there, and he duly arrived for the opening performance. He had never been to Madrid, so I was able to give him something of a guided tour, taking him to all the places I knew well. I also introduced him to the great Spanish dancer Pilar Lopez, who had become a good friend. My dancing in Madrid, whatever misgivings I may have had about it, made Maxim think he would like to write a play for me. During our time in Spain we had got to know each other well, and he had learned a lot about my life. He returned to Britain to take part in the 1978 Edinburgh Festival with *Oscar Remembered*, and between May and August he wrote the one-man play *Dance For Gods*, which so far I have not performed. I learned it, and went back to Canada with Maxim in the autumn, hoping to do the play at the Phoenix Theatre, Montreal.

Unfortunately, my confidence was not unduly strong at that time. The more I thought about it, the more I felt I did not have the nerve nor the recent experience to take the stage with a one-man play. I had not done straight acting for many years, and I was beset by doubts and fears of the unknown. There would be no opportunity to 'play myself in', no supporting cast. If I undertook to do the play I realised it would just be Me, and I would have to carry the whole show. I agonised over the decision and finally came to the conclusion that I could not tackle such a project at that time. I must leave it until later.

I cancelled the whole thing and returned to London, in a way rather ashamed that I did not have the nerve to attempt it, but upon reflection it was the right thing to do.

Undaunted by my decision, Maxim Mazumdar went on to write another play for me, based on my life and called *Invitation to the Dance*, which he wanted me to perform in Newfoundland and later elsewhere. Meanwhile my right leg had been giving me a lot of trouble, and after a visit to my surgeon in December 1979 it was decided that the best solution was for me to have a plastic artery inserted in that leg also, similar to the one I already had in the left leg. I entered hospital, where I spent Christmas, and the operation was successfully performed. When I recovered sufficiently I went to Newfoundland to meet the other two members of the cast of *Invitation to the Dance* – Terri Snelgrove and Jeff Pitcher, returning at the end of February.

Shortly afterwards another opportunity came my way. Lindsay Kemp invited me to go to Italy to play Oberon in his production of

Midsummer Night's Dream, which I very much wanted to do, as it would provide yet more experience for me as a straight actor, bearing in mind I had done no acting since I was a teenager. I gladly accepted the invitation and was due to leave for Italy on 20th March.

It seemed that Fates had not yet finished with me. My bags were packed, my flight was booked, and I thought I was on my way to sunny Italy . . . . It was not to be. Literally twenty-four hours before I was due to leave I was aware that all was not well with my right leg. It began to go cold from the knee downwards. It seemed unbelievable, but I recognised the danger signs immediately and only too well. I wondered what could possibly have happened, as it was only three months since the operation. It was quite frightening, but I tried to push the terrifying portents to the back of my mind. The next morning, the day I was to leave for Italy, I got out of bed to discover to my horror that I could not walk on my leg. I realised then there was no question of my going anywhere. I could not stand, let alone travel to Italy. It was a terrifying realisation, but I knew I had to do something quickly.

I telephoned my surgeon, who fortunately happened to be in London that day, and told him my leg was dead from the knee downwards and I could not walk. Just an hour later he turned up in his car and rushed me to the Nuffield Hospital for emergency surgery. This time it really was touch and go. The plastic artery graft had blocked below the knee, restricting circulation. The fact that the leg had only recently been operated on, plus the hazard that this was the third operation on that leg made it a difficult and delicate piece of surgery, but again my leg was saved. The gravity of this operation was evident by the length of time it took for me to recover. For six weeks I could hardly walk, and the pain was intense at times. I hobbled about on crutches, which I eventually discarded, and made up my mind that somehow I was going to get to Newfoundland to do the play. Having missed out the first time I knew I either had to do it or allow the whole opportunity to go by.

There was a slow gradual improvement, but I knew everybody was very worried about my undertaking the play. Friends were looking at me, seeing my incapacity and knowing the pain, and it was quite clear that everyone thought I was deluding myself if I really believed I could do a series of performances of a play in which I was on stage throughout. Nobody wished to discourage me, and I could see them smiling benignly as they asked casually – or as casually as they could – 'But will your legs be all right?' I saw my surgeon in May and asked him if I was fit to fly, and to my relief he said he thought the venture might be the best mental tonic I could have. That was all I needed, so off I went.

It was the first time I had been to the summer school at Stephenville in Newfoundland, of which Maxim Mazumdar was the guiding light. I found myself faced with a heavy schedule. In addition to rehearsing my own play I was teaching movement to drama students, only three months after my operation. All of this meant that I was on my feet most of the time, and at times I was in great discomfort, but I was determined to go on. There was to be no turning back this time. I was naturally very nervous about getting back on stage myself in what was an extremely exacting role, but it was a wonderful vehicle for my re-entry into the straight theatre. As the whole play was based on my own life I was, in effect, playing myself under the character's name of Jonathan Arden. The other two actors played all the other people who had been involved with me since childhood – my parents, my teachers and other members of that unique club, The Ballet. *Invitation to the Dance* proved to be a great success. A year later I had the opportunity to play with the Lindsay Kemp Company in Italy, and play the role I had to turn down earlier – Oberon in *A Midsummer Night's Dream*.

I had seen Lindsay's company perform, and had admired him for many years. He had been an 'extra' in *Petrouchka* when we first mounted it at Festival Hall. At that time he was a student with Rambert, but has now made his name as a unique artist in the theatre. Working with him was a mad, bizarre experience, and his *Midsummer Night's Dream* unlike anyone else's production of the play, but it was wonderful to be in it, and to perform it in beautiful Italy.

On my way back from Newfoundland in 1980 I had passed through New York, where I showed a copy of *Invitation to the Dance* to freelance producer Kevin Gebhard. He was fascinated by it, and came to St John's to see it performed in September 1980, as a result of which arrangements were put in hand for a New York production in the autumn of 1981, which I have just completed. Gradually, perhaps imperceptibly, my direction is changing, and although I will always be involved with the ballet, the doors are opening into other spheres. Back in Newfoundland in 1981 I played '*Oh Coward*,' the revue based on Noël Coward's works, and that was another fresh experience.

As I look back, I realise that half a century has passed since I came into the world, dancing my way around it for so much of that time. Was there a plan, a formula worked out for me, to which I had to adhere in order to learn? What has it all meant, and where am I going from here? I wonder whether those prophesies will come true, and if the second part of my life will indeed be more important than the first.

How often when growing up one is only concerned with oneself – not unnaturally. There is the question of ambition, and what one hopes to attain. Whether that elusive thing called Perfection is ever reached I shall never know. If it were, there would be no point in existing. One has to work to achieve anything in life; it does not come free. My satisfaction has always been in trying to attain a goal, to give pleasure and beauty to others. I would like to think I have gone a little of the way towards perfection in my art, although Fate cut short that journey perhaps a little too early. Yet I am convinced there was a reason to which at the time I was blind. In the play based on my life there is a passage in which I am told I have always had things too easily – I have simply capitalised on a natural talent, and therefore I did not have to work as hard as others. Now my dancing has gone there are other goals, other things to give. It was so easy to lapse into bitterness and self-pity, but now suddenly the mists seem to be lifting and the light begins to pierce through. My experience has to be passed on to younger generations growing up, in the same way as those great teachers passed on their knowledge and artistry to me. There is no monopoly of art or beauty – we are but caretakers. Our obligation is to hand it on as payment for what we have been given.

My whole being is now poised on the brink of what promises to be a wonderful and exciting adventure, and I must reach out and grasp what comes with all my strength. A new chapter is beginning, and tomorrow is another day. May I be granted the patience and the life force to witness that next chapter, and experience, with gratitude and understanding, all those other tomorrows.

INDEX